PAINTER AND POET

LONDON : HUMPHREY MILFORD

OXFORD UNIVERSITY PRESS

GAINSBOROUGH.   A COUNTRY CHURCHYARD

From an aquatint by Maria C. Prestal, 1790, published in honour of Sir Joshua Reynolds

PAINTER AND POET

Studies in the Literary Relations of English Painting

THE CHARLES ELIOT NORTON LECTURES FOR 1937–1938

BY

CHAUNCEY BREWSTER TINKER

CAMBRIDGE

HARVARD UNIVERSITY PRESS

1938

PRINTED AT THE HARVARD UNIVERSITY PRESS

CAMBRIDGE, MASS., U. S. A.

ELIZABETH WHEELER MANWARING

Quondam discipulae
Nuper magistrae

PREFACE

I HAVE been at no great pains to rid these essays of the atmosphere of the lecture-room, since it is well-nigh impossible to transform such public addresses into scholarly monographs. The treatment of my subject was from the beginning meant to be suggestive rather than closely defined; and in thus disclaiming any dogmatic intention, I have had no choice, because I make no pretension to the rôle of art-critic. The reader will find here no pronouncements regarding the technical merits of pictures and but little use of terms such as composition, draughtsmanship, impasto, and tactile values. Many of the pictures of which I speak are perhaps of no very high degree of artistic worth, but none of them, I think, is negligible if considered as an exponent of the civilization that produced it. In writing of the relation of pictures to poetry and of their usefulness to the historian of literature, I have at least the high authority of Professor Norton, in whose honour the chair of poetry in Harvard University was named. His first course of lectures there, sixty-four years ago, was entitled 'The History of the Fine Arts in their relation to Literature.'

Painters have sometimes laughed at laymen presumptuous enough to express opinions about an art which they were incapable of practising; but the retort may be made that the only painter whose criticism — say of Reynolds — is worth having is one who can himself paint better than Sir Joshua. The seven artists here discussed certainly did not address their work exclusively to their professional associates; indeed, most of them would have assented without a moment's hesitation to Reynolds's dictum, 'It is not the eye, it is the mind which the painter of genius desires to address.'

To mention by name all those who have assisted me by criticism and suggestion would make this book seem more ambitious than I am willing it should appear. Those to whom I am most indebted for encouragement are aware already of the depth of my gratitude, for they know that without their stimulus my task could never have been brought to completion. I have attempted to make special acknowledgement in my text of those to whom I am indebted for information freely given me in my need, and to those who have made it possible for me to see pictures privately owned. The officers and staff of the Fogg Museum in Harvard University and the professors in the Department of the Fine Arts received me with a generous courtesy in the best tradition of academic hospitality — a grace which, happily, shows no sign of disappearing from American universities. I can only wish that this book were a worthier response to the honour shown me in Cambridge.

C. B. T.

Yale University, August 29, 1938

ACKNOWLEDGEMENTS

For the reproduction of pictures in their possession I am indebted to His Majesty, the King of England; the Duke of Buccleuch; the Marquess of Cholmondeley; Lady Desborough; Lord Faringdon; Captain Ford; Mrs. Robert Homans; the Duke of Manchester; Sir Edward Marsh; J. P. Morgan, Esq.; A. Edward Newton, Esq.; Lord Sackville; the Duke of Sutherland; Lord Tollemache; William Ziegler, Esq.; and to the authorities of the Boston Museum of Fine Arts, the Foundling Hospital, the Fitzwilliam Museum, the Frick Collection, the Gallery of Fine Arts of Yale University, the Huntington Art Gallery, the National Gallery, the National Portrait Gallery, St. Bartholomew's Hospital, the Tate Gallery, and the Victoria and Albert Museum.

CONTENTS

ILLUSTRATIONS

PAINTER AND POET

POETIC PAINTING IN ENGLAND

IN December of the year 1746, there issued from the press of
Andrew Millar in London a modest volume entitled, *Odes on
Several Descriptive and Allegorical Subjects*, by William Collins. It
contained but twelve poems, various in metrical form, but all more
or less Greek in manner. The title-page bore a quotation from
Pindar, in which the poet prayed for the gift of audacity and
power (δύναμις) in serving the Muse. The poems were for the most
part addressed to abstractions, Fear, Simplicity, Pity, and the
like — subjects which could hardly prove to be popular even in the
mid-eighteenth century when reflective poetry was more highly
regarded than it is to-day. The little book was ere long suppressed
by its sensitive and unhappy author; but, like many another, he
had despaired too quickly, for it was destined to give him a per-
manent place in the history of English literature; and two of the
poems, 'How sleep the brave?' and the unrhymed 'Ode to Evening,' were to take rank among the finest lyrics in the language. It
is not of these, however, that I wish to speak, but rather of the allegorical odes in the volume, and of these, not because of their cool,
Parian beauty, but for the significant utterances about the art of
poetry which they contain, and which a critic would do well to heed.

William Collins was a young graduate of Oxford, with a passionate desire to write — a familiar type — eager, but hypersensi-
tive, and endowed with a vein of poetry which, though slender,
was very definitely golden. He was, even according to eighteenth
century standards, learned; he was well acquainted with both the
ancients and the moderns. His views of the history of poetry were
similar to those which Thomas Gray was presently to express in his
ode on the 'Progress of Poesy.' He was aware, moreover, that in
1746 the condition of poetry in England was not satisfactory: the
sounds were forced, the notes were few. There was needed

more of strength, diviner rage
Than all which charms this laggard age,

a baptism of fire — the gift of audacity, passion, wonder, that very δύναμις for which Pindar had prayed centuries before.

About half the allegorical odes deal with this theme, the nature, art, and needs of poetry; and one of them — Collins's most difficult poem — is actually entitled, 'Ode on the Poetical Character'; moreover, the odes to Pity, Fear, Mercy, and Simplicity deal with these abstract qualities chiefly as related to the art of poetry; since the passions are conceived of as handmaidens of the Muse, humble attendants in her train. Thus in the 'Ode to Simplicity' the subject is throughout 'the powers of song,' and the charm that simplicity adds to them:

> Though taste, though genius bless
> To some divine excess,
> Faints the cold work till Thou inspire the whole.

Here is a very theory of poetry, a swift analysis of its qualities. The demands upon the poet are four: he must have *taste*, a knowledge of the technique and the conventions of his art; *genius*, by which I suppose originality to be meant; a 'divine *excess*,' called by Collins elsewhere a rage and a 'wild, enthusiast heat,' and by Shakespeare the poet's 'fine frenzy'; and, last and most important of all, without which the whole work remains cold and lifeless, *simplicity*. Whatever may be thought of his analysis, it is clear that the author desired a change from the prevailing standards. His emphasis on passion, that 'divine excess,' and on simplicity, hardly strikes what is commonly thought of as the eighteenth century note. So in the 'Ode to Fear':

> O Thou whose spirit most possest
> The sacred seat of Shakespear's breast!
> By all that from thy prophet broke,
> In thy divine emotions spoke:
> Hither again thy fury deal,
> Teach me but once like him to feel:
> His cypress wreath my meed decree,
> And I, O Fear, will dwell with thee!

This, then, was the advanced poetic position before the full noon of the Romantic Movement. Against it I propose to project certain events, tendencies, and persons in the history of English painting, since the two arts were closely related, and are mutually interpretative.

But Collins's views on this subject are even more explicitly stated in his early *Epistle to Sir Thomas Hanmer on his Edition of Shakespear's Works*. An unpromising title, is it not? — appropriate enough to one of those dull tissues of hypocritical compliment which have brought the poetry of the eighteenth century into disrepute, and of which the modern reader is content to remain ignorant. But in this, as in all Collins's poems, there is something significant. In this epistle he suggests that Poetry might well seek the assistance of Painting:

> O might the Muse with equal ease persuade
> Expressive Picture to adopt thine aid,
> Some powerful Raphael should again appear,
> And arts consenting fix their empire here.[1]

The poet then paints two imaginary pictures: the grief of Mark Antony over the body of Caesar; and Coriolanus confronted by his suppliant mother at the gates of Rome. Shakespeare, you see, is to inspire the painter of historic pictures, and, in return, to receive new lustre from him:

> The sister Arts shall nurse their drooping fires,
> Each from his scenes her stores alternate bring,
> Spread the fair tints, or wake the vocal string.[2]

These words were printed a quarter of a century before the Royal Academy was founded, and nearly half a century before the opening of Boydell's Shakespeare Gallery. The names of Reynolds and Gainsborough were as yet unknown: Reynolds, at the age of twenty, was a pupil under Hudson, and had not yet begun his studies in Italy; Gainsborough was a boy of sixteen, from a distant

---

[1] The passage is quoted from the first edition of 1743; the words were somewhat altered in the second edition, though the sentiment remained the same.

[2] This view of the relation of the two arts re-appears in the 'Ode to Pity'; to her the poet would fain erect a temple:

> There Picture's toils shall well relate
> How chance or hard-involving Fate
>   O'er mortal bliss prevail:
> The buskined Muse shall near her stand,
> And sighing prompt her tender hand
>   With each disastrous tale.

village in Suffolk. What would Collins have thought, had he known that his wish was to be granted, that the art of painting was about to rise to its glorious zenith, that the leader of the English School was to express again and again the doctrine that the various arts all represented one aspiration of the spirit, and that painting and poetry were so closely akin as to be interdependent?

And now we are confronted by the significant question, Do the paintings of the English School illustrate the qualities which Collins regarded as essential in poetry? At first sight, certainly not. If we are to discover simplicity and divine excess, for example, we must look painstakingly for them, and in the end may feel that our search has not been very successful; but we are to remember that originality, passion, and simplicity are not easily attained by an artist whose chief business is the painting of portraits. As a class dependent on the gentry, English painters gave themselves to the rather unexciting task of transmitting to posterity the admirable but monotonous likenesses of the well-to-do. When one's task is to produce a 'speaking likeness,' it is difficult to submit oneself to the divine fire. Even at its best, portraiture foregoes whole sections of human life. The emaciation of the sick, the ecstasy of the martyr, the convulsive mischief of comedy, the pity and terror of tragedy, failure, ruin, and death — from all these the portrait-painter is cut off. Before sitting for our portrait, we await a moment when the woe of life and most of its passion decline to a mere vestige or a fading memory.

For the English painter there was no other means of subsistence than portraiture. He was the inheritor of a tradition of subservience which, coming down through a succession of court-painters, had impressed its character upon English art. Unless a painter could devise some novel means of appealing to the middle classes, as did Hogarth, there was no other way of getting a livelihood than by entering into the servitude of portrait-painting. For ecclesiastical painting there was no demand, since the national Church was prejudiced against the use of such material symbols as pictures and images. The minatory tables of the law, the Ten Commandments in black and gold, were deemed the proper embellishment for the altars of the Most High. Landscape was slowly rising in favour, but confronted a sluggish and indifferent world: why hang up pictures of the English countryside when you could look out of the window? Still life had never established itself in England as a worthy branch of painting: why buy pictures of fruit or fish when you could buy the commodity itself? Genre-painting, save in the form of sporting pictures, hardly existed. Fresco and historical paintings were in occasional demand, but so irregularly that they afforded no sure means of subsistence. How, moreover, were they to be shown to the public? Pictures of all kinds might indeed be painted, but how were they to be sold?

Moreover, when the painter, in defiance of the current demand and the public taste, painted in these forbidden manners, he was liable to ludicrous failure. When one aspires to originality and 'a divine excess,' one's audacity will probably be matched by one's disappointment. Even to-day the attempts of the eighteenth century artists to escape from the conventions are generally treated with derision. In the course of these remarks I shall have occasion to comment on many pictures which, I suppose, must be called ridiculous rather than sublime; but which are, for that very reason, related to our immediate subject, the attempt of the painters to escape from the prevalent styles.

The four portraits which will presently be considered betray this desire to escape, and may fairly be called 'poetical,' since they reveal certain of the characteristics which Collins believed to be the genuine marks of poetry. All four are notable chiefly for the subject, and as subject-pieces first came into notice. The fame of the pictures arose not from the gorgeous originals, glowing with light and colour, but from prints in black and white. None of the originals was accessible to the public, since all were privately owned; three of the portraits, when completed, were engraved, and the fourth would have been engraved also, but for a quarrel between the sitter and the artist.[1] Prints of the kind became intensely popular.[2] Painters were naturally glad to have a memory of their pictures preserved by such reproductions, and the engrav-

[1] The portrait of Garrick and his wife was not engraved until the nineteenth century; the first public acquaintance with the portrait was in the printed form.

[2] See *The English Print*, by Basil Gray, London, 1937; and E. W. Manwaring, *Italian Landscape in 18th Century England*, New York, 1925, especially pp. 76–86.

ers of Great Britain thus found lucrative employment, until at last pictures were often painted in order that they might be engraved. A logical, though quixotic, approach to the great English painters of the eighteenth century may be made through these engraved plates, which have a beauty all their own. Mezzotints, aquatints, and other prints were feverishly collected by connoisseurs. Print-shops abounded. Both Macklin's Gallery of paintings illustrative of the British Poets and Boydell's Shakespeare Gallery were made possible by the income derived from the sale of prints of the paintings there displayed. Horace Walpole's collection of prints, probably the largest in England, was famous. Sir Joshua Reynolds kept a portfolio of prints in his rooms in Leicester Fields, so that clients awaiting an appointment might not only have opportunity for a pleasant pastime, but come into his studio with some notion of his manner, or even with suggestions for the embellishment of their own portraits. In his discourses before the Royal Academy he used prints as illustrative material, and recommended their study:

> We may in a great measure supply the deficiency which I mentioned — of not having his [Michael Angelo's] works so perpetually before our eyes — by having recourse to . . . drawings or even copies of those drawings; to prints, which, however ill executed, still convey something by which this taste may be formed, and a relish may be fixed and established in our minds for this grand style of invention. Some examples of this kind we have in the Academy; and I sincerely wish there were more, that the younger students might in their first nourishment imbibe this taste.[1]

Observe that Sir Joshua believes not only that the study of prints is an appropriate and useful approach to the study of painting, but also that 'taste' may be thus imbibed.

In these four examples the marks of originality, passion, and simplicity will not be at once apparent, since these traits are easily obscured by the prevailing conventions which no artist, however ardently he may attempt to do so, quite succeeds in evading. But, even within the narrow bounds of portraiture, a painter's desire for another and a freer manner may betray itself. In spite of the

---

[1] Discourse XV.

restrictions of tradition and of public demand, painters gradually
enlarged their scope, and the imagination, or 'fancy,' as it was
commonly called, had opportunity to express itself. The result
was an increase in the number of portraits of persons outside the
ranks of the gentry: actors and actresses, courtesans, peasants,
children, soldiers and sailors, foreigners, huntsmen, and people
garbed for masquerade, for sport, or for the intimacies of domestic
life. Association with such sitters enabled artists to indulge the
imagination, if not to a 'divine excess,' yet in pleasant excitement
at having evaded a tyrannous routine.[1]

Now when a painter feels this need of release from commonplace patrons, what more inspiring sitter can he have than a play-
actor? and what player ever furnished portrait-painters with a
greater variety of pose and manner than did David Garrick? To
which of them shall we turn for the most characteristic likeness of
him? to Hogarth, or Reynolds, or Gainsborough, or Zoffany, or
Pine? Their varied skill has failed to leave us a full record of the
man, though there are pictures of him in comic and in tragic rôles;
on the stage, and in the green room; in the society of the great and
gay, and among his professional associates; taking his ease in his
villa on the banks of the Thames, and standing in a park, pre-
tentiously embracing a marble bust of Shakespeare. One portrait
— and that not the most bizarre — depicts him seated at his writing desk, engaged in literary work, but interrupted by his charming young wife, Eva Violette. Hogarth painted this at the height
of his powers; and it is clear that he aimed to avoid the stiffness so
often felt in portraits, and attempted to catch, as it were, a moment
in the life of his two friends, a delightful 'instant made eternity.'
The canvas seems to have been finished about 1757, though exactly when the sittings were begun is a matter for conjecture.
Garrick is not yet forty years of age. His wife, a former dancer,
seven years his junior, he had married in 1749. But what is going
on? The author, pen in hand, is lost in meditation, for he is com-
posing a prologue, a kind of verse in which he excelled, so that he
won the praise of Samuel Johnson (himself a writer of prologues)
for having produced more good ones than even the great Dryden.

[1] See the note by Opie at the end of this chapter.

He is represented as at work upon the prologue for a farce-comedy called *Taste* (1752), by his friend, Samuel Foote. The play ridiculed the fashionable craze for Continental *objets d'art*, and particularly for blistered pictures and mutilated statues; it may very well have been suggested by Hogarth's own ridicule of such folly in his picture entitled 'Taste in High Life,' [1] and in the second and third plates of his 'Marriage à la Mode'; for the pugnacious little painter never wearied of decrying the notion that Englishmen had anything to learn from the Continent or from the past. So the portrait of Garrick had, from its inception, a very definitely literary flavour, and a twofold relation to the man who painted it.

Hogarth has represented the actor's wife as stealing up behind him, to seize the pen which he holds poised in air; but I think the spectator is supposed to guess that Garrick is not unaware of the lady's presence; for he, as we know on good authority, never ceased acting, least of all when he was off the stage, and I suggest that he is here merely pretending to meditate. In charm he certainly yields to Eva, who is Hogarth's loveliest female figure, a vision in pink and white tulle.

There is a story that the actor made some criticism of the expression of his countenance — perhaps as lacking in vivacity — and that the angry painter drew his wet brush across the eyes, and thus destroyed the value of his work. It is said to bear signs of re-painting, but by what hand is unknown. The picture remained in the possession of the artist's widow until her death, when, at the Hogarth Sale, it was purchased by Edward Locker, who later sold it to King George IV. It has remained in the royal collection ever since, and, though shown at the great exhibition of the English School in 1934, is seldom seen by the public, who thus lack a first-hand acquaintance with Hogarth's most poetic portrait.

Five years after the painting of this portrait, Reynolds exhibited at the annual show of the Incorporated Society of Artists (1762) his startling picture of 'Garrick between Tragedy and Comedy.' [2] It was at once handsomely engraved in mezzotint by

[1] A surreptitious print of it appeared in 1746.
[2] The canvas is now in the possession of Edward Rothschild, Esq.

HOGARTH. GARRICK AND HIS WIFE

From the portrait in Windsor Castle

Edward Fisher, but, instead of its present title, bore the words, 'Reddere personae scit convenientia cuique' — a sentiment which must have had the approval of both painter and actor as expressing the meaning of the picture. One might think of Comedy as likely to win the contest for the player's allegiance; but Garrick continued his devotion to both kinds of drama throughout his career. With this portrait Reynolds entered the realm of the imagination, for it represents a living person, as well-known as anybody in London, standing between two allegorical figures who are striving to draw him in opposite directions. Neither of the Muses — for such they are — can be enthusiastically praised, and it is difficult to believe that any human being could have posed for the wooden figure of Tragedy. Comedy has a more natural, though somewhat kittenish, expression.[1] In the famous picture of Mrs. Siddons as the 'Tragic Muse,' painted nearly a quarter of a century later, Reynolds again introduced two attendant allegorical personages, usually called Crime and Remorse,[2] but they fade into the background, and were hardly meant for more than suggestive shadows. It would perhaps have been wise to adopt a somewhat different treatment of Tragedy and Comedy; but one cannot wish them wholly out of the way, unless one is willing to sacrifice the entire picture. That would indeed be a loss, since this is the liveliest of all the portraits of the actor, a truly interpretative picture, such as used to be called a 'psychological' portrait.

How, one might ask, could Reynolds have conveyed his meaning in any other way? He wished to depict the two contending passions in Garrick's nature, his infectious love of hilarity and his vaulting ambition to excel in the supreme form of drama. How, without representing an actual stage-scene, could the painter have caught the histrionic Garrick, which, when all is said, one must regard as the essential Garrick? Contrast this with numerous later portraits in which he is painted as he appeared in ordinary life,

[1] The model for 'Comedy' is sometimes said to have been Sir Joshua's niece, Theophila Palmer, but she was only five years old when the picture was painted. See Leslie and Taylor, vol. I, p. 205. Nor is there any satisfactory evidence that it was Mrs. Abington who posed.

[2] Since the first holds a poisoned bowl, and the other a scourge.

REYNOLDS. GARRICK BETWEEN TRAGEDY AND COMEDY

From an engraving by Edward Fisher, 1762

and this picture will be seen to be no mere portrait, but a poetic characterisation.[1]

It will hardly do, I think, to assert, as does the latest of Sir Joshua's critics, 'He was at his best when at his most simple, and in his single figures.'[2] This pronouncement is true, no doubt, as indicating that which the advance guard of contemporary critics will deign to tolerate; it may even define that portion of the artist's work which is likely to survive longest; but it must never be forgotten that Reynolds aspired to something more than the record of masculine dignity and of feminine charm. He was no less proud of his 'poetic' painting, his fancy-pieces which displayed his peculiar skill in dramatising a person or casting him, as it were, in an imaginary rôle. It was by such means, and by such alone, that he could successfully transcend the limitations imposed by portrait-painting.

He himself admitted the artificiality of this process, but defended it, and drew a distinction between the 'greater truth' and the lesser. He differentiates the 'larger and more liberal idea of Nature from the narrow and confined; that which addresses itself to the imagination from that which is solely addressed to the eye,' and adds,

> It must be remembered that this great style itself is artificial in the highest degree; it presupposes in the spectator a cultivated and prepared, artificial state of mind.[3]

It is on this theory that the 'fancy' portraits of Reynolds are conceived; but they must not be thought of as in any way peculiar to him or to the English School. It was a fine old convention of portrait-painting, which extended back, through Kneller and Lely, to Van Dyck and to Rubens. Most of us are acquainted with Van Dyck's portrait of himself in youth, half nude, holding a shepherd's crook;[4] and every visitor to Hampton Court for the last

---

[1] Since writing the above, I have come upon the following in John Britton's *The Fine Art of the English School*, 1812, regarding this portrait of 'Garrick between Tragedy and Comedy': 'This may be called a poetical portrait or an historical allegory: a living character constitutes the subject of the composition, but this is embellished by the fancy of the artist.' (Pp. 51–52.)

[2] The anonymous author of the preface to the catalogue of the Reynolds Exhibition, London, 1936.

[3] Discourse XV.   [4] In the Wallace Collection.

two hundred years has seen the whole heaven of ladies painted by Lely as goddesses and saints. The French School also furnishes admirable examples in this kind. How familiar it all was in the eighteenth century is shown by the amusing words of Charles Surface, when, in the fourth act of *The School for Scandal*, he auctioned off the portraits of his ancestors:

'Here, now, is a maiden sister of his, my great-aunt Deborah, done by Kneller, in his best manner, and esteemed a very formidable likeness. There she is, you see, a shepherdess feeding her flock. You shall have her for five pounds ten — the sheep are worth the money.'

To the first exhibition of the Royal Academy (1769) the President sent four pictures, three of which were in this 'great' or fanciful style: 'Mrs. Blake receiving the Girdle of Venus,'[1] Miss Morris as 'Hope nursing Love' (a charming fantasy of a young woman suckling an infant Cupid), and the Duchess of Manchester as 'Diana stealing his Bow from Cupid.' Such were the *morceaux de réception* by which Reynolds was fain to illustrate his leadership of the English School.

The picture of the Duchess of Manchester as Diana, which is still in the possession of the family, was lent by the present Duke to the great exhibition of Reynolds's work held in London in 1936. In its engraved form — for a print by Watson was published in 1766, even before the canvas itself was exhibited — it is highly valued by collectors. It is easy to forget that this is a portrait of a mother and her three-year-old child, George, Viscount Mandeville, and to think of it instead as a poetic, if rather preposterous, picture. It reminds us once more of the words of Charles Surface who laughs at the 'modern Raphaels' — who, pray, but Reynolds and Romney? — 'who give you the strongest resemblance, yet contrive to make your portrait independent of you; so that you may sink the original, and not hurt the picture.' One would have difficulty in forgetting (sinking) this picture, but no one would ever recall it as a lady's portrait.

If this canvas illustrates that warmth of the imagination which Collins idealised, it also reveals, oddly enough, the desire for sim-

---

[1] Suggested of course by Italian pictures of St. Thomas receiving the girdle of the Virgin at the Assumption.

A. C. Cooper & Sons

REYNOLDS.   DIANA DISARMING CUPID

From the painting in the possession of the Duke of Manchester

plicity which should accompany it. The painter has rid himself of the problem of modern attire by representing the Duchess in long, flowing robes, such as he later commended in his fourth Discourse:

It requires the nicest judgment to dispose the drapery so that the folds shall have an easy communication, and gracefully follow each other, with such natural negligence as to look like the effect of chance, and at the same time show the figure under it to the utmost advantage.

Diana is without jewels or other adornment save the crescent above her forehead; her hair is simply dressed; she is shod with sandals, and her little boy lies on the ground in all the simplicity of the nude, save for a pair of wings to indicate his celestial origin.

The ridiculousness of certain of these 'fancy' pictures did not escape attention. One account, satiric enough, is familiar to every reader of *The Vicar of Wakefield*. It will be remembered that when the Primrose family felt themselves to be rising in the world, they decided to be painted in a large family group, not without allegorical graces:

My wife [says the Vicar of Wakefield] desired to be represented as Venus, and the painter was instructed not to be too frugal of his diamonds in her stomacher and hair. Her two little ones were to be as Cupids by her side; while I, in my gown and band, was to present her with my books on the Whistonian controversy. [1]

Except for the reference to the Whistonian controversy, this description of the Primrose portrait is hardly exaggerated, and must be fairly representative of the demands made upon Sir Joshua day by day. The *Vicar* was published in 1766, the very year in which Reynolds began work on the Duchess's picture. But it is characteristic of Goldsmith to carry his humour to the limit of the ludicrous, and his description of the family picture is continued till it becomes sheer caricature:

Olivia would be drawn as an Amazon, sitting upon a bank of flowers, dressed in a green joseph, richly laced with gold, and a whip in her hand. Sophia was to be a shepherdess, with as many sheep as the painter could put in for nothing; and Moses was to be dressed out with a hat and

---

[1] Chapter XVI.

white feather. Our taste so much pleased the squire, that he insisted on being put in as one of the family, in the character of Alexander the Great, at Olivia's feet.

But amusement over these pictures may be carried too far, for some of them are beautiful. Reynolds's masterpiece in this kind is, I think, 'Lady Bunbury sacrificing to the Graces,' a large canvas now in the Chicago gallery. Its glowing colour has long since faded — Reynolds's portraits, it was said, aged more rapidly than did the sitters — but the outlines are as lovely as ever, and the subject highly characteristic of the age, a symbol of stateliness and grace.

Sir Joshua never abandoned this poetic style. As late as 1787, he painted Mrs. Billington, a popular soprano of the day, as St. Cecilia singing among the clouds, surrounded by *amorini*.[1] Two of these fancy or 'subject' pieces have retained their popularity down to our own time: Mrs. Sheridan seated at the organ, as St. Cecilia (1775), assisted by two cherubs singing at her side; and Mrs. Siddons enthroned as the Tragic Muse. In this manner Reynolds was, as in other respects, the leading painter of his time, and without a serious rival. Gainsborough was not disposed to compete with him in this kind of picture, since he found diversion from 'face-painting' elsewhere. His landscapes, not his portraits, represent his poetic manner. Romney, however, who followed the great President in many ways, imitated him also in this. He painted his own 'Tragic Muse' (1771),[2] with Mrs. Yates, a popular actress, in the title-rôle, reminiscent of 'Lady Bunbury sacrificing to the Graces'; it is well-known as a print, for it was engraved by Valentine Green. Romney painted Mrs. Yates again, with serene indifference to gender, as 'Il Penseroso' (to Mrs. Jordan's 'L'Allegro'); and drew two subjects from Hayley's dull poem, *The Triumphs of Temper*, which show Serena reading Miss Burney's *Evelina*.[3] Under the immediate inspiration of Emma Hamilton, he produced charming portraits of Ariadne, Cassandra, Miranda, Medusa, and a Bacchante, with a score of other likenesses, in-

[1] In the New York Public Library.

[2] The picture is not influenced by 'Mrs. Siddons as the Tragic Muse,' which was not painted till 1786.

[3] One of the two pictures is in the Huntington Gallery at San Marino.

cluding 'Comedy' in 'Tragedy and Comedy nursing the Infant Shakespeare.'

Romney's sweet and idealistic nature gave ready expression to smooth and glowing dreams, and his happy pencil bestowed nobility upon his men and the fashionable 'sensibility' upon his women. Vigour and passion (in divine excess) it was not his to depict, but grace and simplicity. His picture of the Stafford children,[1] often called 'Children dancing in a Ring,' is perhaps Romney's masterpiece; the place of honour was assigned to it in the Burlington Exhibition of 1934, and rightly, if we esteem the spirit of the age which produced it; for nothing could be more characteristic of the late eighteenth century. It has the stateliness and simplicity of a minuet by Handel; and I think Collins might have found in it an emblem of his own lines about Simplicity:

> Thou who, with hermit heart,
> Disdain'st the wealth of art,
> And gauds and pageant weeds, and trailing pall,
> But com'st a decent Maid,
> In Attic robe array'd,
> O chaste, unboastful Nymph, to thee I call!

The picture combines the rhythm of the dance with the gayety of childhood, and rejects the ostentation of the British gentry, enrobed in court-attire, with decorations on the breast, and evidence of high birth everywhere apparent (seen even in the backgrounds of the more elaborate portraits, where the extensive prospect is itself a boastful assertion of great possessions). Romney here contents himself with the simple sport of young children and an elder sister 'in Attic robe array'd.'

What has here been said about the interest attaching to such poetic paintings as these need not modify in any degree our esteem for Reynolds and Romney as portrait-painters. The immortal likenesses of Goldsmith, Sterne, the Countess of Albemarle, Lord Heathfield, Warren Hastings, John Wesley, and a hundred other simple portraits will best exemplify the hand of the two masters.

---

[1] The offspring of Lord Gower. The girl with the tambourine is the Lady Anne, half-sister to the rest. Granville, the son and heir, is the smallest of the children. The picture was engraved by J. R. Smith in 1781.

But the aberrations of genius have a significance of their own, and to the student of literature a peculiar value; for it is not master-pieces alone which reveal the character and aims of a painter, but his first attempts, rough sketches, trial compositions, rejected designs, and above all, the pictures which he painted in defiance of the public taste to suit himself. Some are beautiful, some ludicrous; and both are too often passed over by historians as of no importance. Such pictures disclose at once the spirit of the age and the protest against it. Some of these I propose to examine, not at all with the intention to show that they are well or ill painted (for I am inadequate to such a task), but rather to see where the artist's interest in mere subject-matter led him and from what peculiar sources he may have derived his inspiration.

All the great portrait-painters of the age (with the possible exception of the Scotchmen, Ramsay and Raeburn) aver frank dissatisfaction with the restrictions imposed upon them by current standards, and seek expression in other ways. Hogarth, the out-spoken, was loud in his protests, and, as the most original of them all, became the first great master of conversation-pieces, and, a little later, the author of a series of moral comedies with which, by means of cheaply-priced engravings, he made a direct appeal to the unpretentious middle classes, who were, in general, of no great interest to portrait-painters. Reynolds found a similar, though less audacious, means of release in fancy-subjects, as did Gains-borough in the genre-paintings which constitute his final manner.

I am persuaded that, in the true estimate of a painter of genius, his eccentricities cannot safely be left unconsidered, since his aberrations are indicative of his aspirations, and aspirations are no less significant than achievements. But however this may be, it is in such questing that the painters most clearly reflect the literary movements of the age in which they live, and become illustrative of it. Thus the arts of painting and poetry enter, as the artists desired that they should, into alliance and harmony, so that the more we know of the one art, the more we shall know of the other also.

ROMNEY. CHILDREN DANCING IN A RING

From the painting in the collection of the Duke of Sutherland

NOTE

Opie, who delighted in fancy-subjects and historical pieces, remarked in his second lecture (1806) as Professor of Painting:

Next to the study of nature, and the fine examples produced by the art itself, reading of various kinds, chiefly of history, natural history, voyages, travels, works of imagination, and, above all, of poetry, in all its branches, may be considered as affording the most copious fund of materials, and imparting the most powerful stimulus to invention.

(*Lectures on Painting by the Royal Academicians*,
London, Henry Bohn, 1848, p. 272.)

In the next paragraph, he asserts that both arts set out from the same place, journey to the same end, and require the same kind of original powers. Later (p. 282), he expresses the resentment against the restrictions imposed by portrait-painting, to which reference has been made above:

So habituated are the people of this country to the sight of portraiture only, that they can scarcely as yet consider painting in any other light; they will hardly admire a landscape that is not a view of a particular place, nor a history unless composed of likenesses of the persons represented; and are apt to be staggered, confounded, and wholly unprepared to follow such vigorous flights of imagination, as would — *as will* be felt and applauded with enthusiasm in a more advanced and liberal state of criticism. In our exhibitions . . . one's ear is pained, one's very soul is sick with hearing crowd after crowd, sweeping round and, instead of discussing the merits of the different works on view (as to conception, composition, and execution), all reiterating the same dull and tasteless question, *Who is that?* and *Is it like?*

II

HOGARTH: THE HUMANITARIAN IMPULSE

IN the year 1728, James Oglethorpe, a member of Parliament, some thirty-two years old, was so horrified by reports of torture inflicted upon prisoners in English jails, and, in particular, by the experiences of a friend imprisoned for debt, as to move that the House of Commons appoint a committee of inquiry. His motion was carried, and he was made chairman of a large group of investigators, who, fortunately, took a serious view of their duties. They began by visiting in a body the famous Fleet Prison, against the Warden of which, Thomas Bambridge, many charges of cruelty were already in circulation. The visitors discovered, among other victims, a baronet, Sir William Rich, half naked and loaded with irons, on whom a special punishment had been inflicted because he was charged with having insulted the Warden. Public indignation ran high, and Bambridge was reported by the committee to have been guilty of 'the most notorious breaches of his trust, extortions, and high crimes and misdemeanours.' [1] He is said narrowly to have escaped being torn in pieces by a London mob.

The prevalent indignation had a more worthy and enduring expression than this. Oddly enough, it was in verse. In 1730 a young Scotch poet, then just rising into fame, James Thomson, introduced into his poem 'Winter' [2] a passage eulogising the members of the committee, who were still engaged in their investigations:

> And here can I forget the generous few,
> Who, touched with human woe, redressive searched
> Into the horrors of the gloomy jail?
> Unpitied and unheard where misery moans;
> Where sickness pines, where thirst and hunger burn,
> And poor misfortune feels the lash of vice . . .

---

[1] For a full account of the investigation and its unsatisfactory sequel, see A. A. Ettinger's *James Oglethorpe*, Oxford University Press, 1937.

[2] Thomson's *Seasons*, edited by J. Logie Robertson, 'Winter,' lines 359 ff. The passage is not in the first edition of 'Winter,' which had appeared separately in 1725.

> Little tyrants raged,
> Snatched the lean morsel from the starving mouth,
> Tore from cold wintry limbs the tattered weed,
> Even robbed them of the last of comforts, sleep,
> The free-born Briton to the dungeon chained
> Or, as the lust of cruelty prevailed,
> At pleasure marked him with inglorious stripes,
> And crushed out lives, by secret barbarous ways,
> That for their country would have toiled or bled. . . .
>
> Ye sons of mercy! yet resume the search;
> Drag forth the legal monsters into light,
> Wrench from their hands Oppression's iron rod,
> And bid the cruel feel the pains they give.

This is not poetry of a very soaring kind, but it reveals the intensity of the new humanitarianism which was to manifest itself in a score of important ways, and nowhere more conspicuously than in the novels of Fielding, Smollett, Goldsmith, and Sterne, each of whom was later to describe prison-life, and so help to spread the new philanthropy and to prepare the way for the great hero of prison-reform, John Howard.

The subject had also its picturesque treatment. A great painter depicted the scene of Bambridge's trial, or rather his examination in the prison, with an appeal more immediate and lively than that of a poet or a novelist. William Hogarth was present at certain meetings of the committee in order to record and perpetuate the dramatic scene. Just how this came about is not known; but it is reasonable to suppose that permission to attend was obtained for him by his father-in-law, Sir James Thornhill, a member of Parliament and of the committee. The finished picture,[1] it may be inferred, was worked up from sketches and notes made on the spot.

The painting shows the committee in session. (Did ever artist, before or since, paint a picture of a committee-meeting?) Bambridge stands at the extreme left, near Oglethorpe, who turns to look up at him. In the centre is one of the victims of the Warden's cruelty, kneeling before his examiners, to show the weight of the enormous irons with which he has been loaded. Another similar instrument of torture is in the hands of a jailer, the fifth figure from

[1] In the National Portrait Gallery.

W. F. Mansell

W. F. Mansell

HOGARTH.   THE EXAMINATION OF BAMBRIDGE

Above: from the painting in the National Portrait Gallery; below: from the oil sketch
in the Fitzwilliam Museum

the left, who pushes the iron towards the chairman, and points an accusing finger at Bambridge, whose lips are parted in a snarl of rage as he shakes his clenched fist at his underling.

Hogarth was in his thirty-second year when this picture was painted, but not yet a well-known artist. None of the great works associated with his name had as yet been produced, and this picture is therefore the more significant as indicating the essential nature of his artistic gifts and the direction in which his work was to develop. Up to this time he had been chiefly concerned with the illustration of books, notably of Butler's *Hudibras* — a kind of work in which he always excelled. But from now on his pictures were to be an expression of his own individuality, and were to set forth the whole *comédie humaine*, as he saw it — amusingly and dramatically, that is, but with frequent emphasis upon its dirt, misery, and crime. Of these his study was to be unflinching, and that it might be accurate he made his way into prison and madhouse, hospital and bridewell, where vice and suffering were to be seen at their worst.

One of his unfinished sketches, made during the prison investigations, and revealing, as his sketches always do, the full vigour of his pencil, was later given to his warm admirer and eulogist, Horace Walpole. The picture, which is now in the Fitzwilliam Museum, differs from the one in the National Portrait Gallery. It is thus described by Walpole in his *Anecdotes of Painting*:[1]

I have a sketch in oil that he gave me, which he intended to engrave. It was done at the time that the House of Commons appointed a committee to enquire into the cruelties exercised on prisoners in the Fleet to extort money from them. The scene is the committee; on the table are the instruments of torture. A prisoner in rags, half starved, appears before them; the poor man has a good countenance that adds to the interest. On the other hand is the inhuman gaoler. It is the very figure that Salvator Rosa would have drawn for Iago in the moment of detection. Villany, fear, and conscience are mixed in, yellow and livid, on his countenance, his lips are contracted by tremor, his face advances as eager to lie, his legs step back as thinking to make his escape; one hand is thrust precipitately into his bosom, the fingers of the other are catching uncertainly at his button-holes. If this was a portrait, it is the most speaking that ever was drawn; if it was not, it is still finer.

[1] Edition of 1828, vol. IV, p. 131.

The two pictures show different witnesses. The kneeling man, loaded with irons, in the canvas at the National Portrait Gallery, is replaced, in the Fitzwilliam sketch, by a standing figure, miserably ragged, but without handcuffs or irons of any sort, to whom Oglethorpe is directing the attention of his committee. The artist must, therefore, have sketched at least two different scenes before leaving the prison.[1]

These pictures of the examination of Bambridge belong to a period in Hogarth's career commonly associated with his conversation-pieces; indeed, by stretching the definition a little, these prison-scenes may themselves be termed 'conversations'— scenes from real life, with a dramatic or narrative interest. Hogarth once described his paintings in this manner a little contemptuously, as produced in his green and salad days, and betraying a style which he later discarded. In his autobiographical sketch he says:

I then married, and commenced painter of small conversation pieces, from twelve to fifteen inches high. This having novelty, succeeded for a few years. But though it gave somewhat more scope to the fancy, was still but a less kind of drudgery.[2]

But the conversation-pieces do not deserve to be thus belittled. The artist speaks of them thus because he wished to fix attention on his moral engravings, his account of which, touched with justifiable pride, is calculated to leave the impression that the earlier manner was abandoned in favour of one both more useful to the public and more worthy of his own powers. But as a matter of fact, Hogarth carried over into the moral paintings and engravings many lessons which he had learned while creating the 'conversations'; and to that earlier style of painting he returned more than once in later days. To-day these early domestic paintings enjoy a high popularity.

This popularity reached a climax eight years ago, in the exhibition of such paintings held in London, which was followed by Mr. Sacheverell Sitwell's pleasant book, *Conversation Pieces* (1936). Hogarth's leadership in this peculiarly English art is there set

[1] Further evidence of his visits to prison is found in his two portraits of an infamous murderess, Sarah Malcolm, in 1733, while she was awaiting execution.

[2] Ireland, *Hogarth Illustrated from his own Manuscripts*, vol. III, p. 24.

forth. Some fifteen of Hogarth's oil paintings had been shown in the exhibition, and popular interest in them was stimulated on both sides of the Atlantic; in New York by the exhibition, at the Messrs. Knoedler's gallery, of 'The Lady's Last Stake' from Mr. Morgan's collection, and the 'Wedding of Mr. Stephen Becking-ham,' since acquired by the Metropolitan Museum; and in London by the addition to the National Gallery of the artist's amusing portrait of the 'Graham Children at Play.'

Some of these have a beauty of sentiment and a harmony of colour not always associated with the name of Hogarth. In the picture of the Beckingham Wedding there is even a fanciful detail that must cause great distress to those who think of the artist merely as a brilliant realist. Above the heads of the bride and groom hover a group of *putti* or *amorini*, discharging the contents of a cornucopia of fruit and flowers. These cherubic attendants are Hogarth's concession to 'poetic' painting, and are in odd but not unpleasant contrast to two inquisitive human beings who look down upon the scene from a balcony.

Humour is seldom absent from these conversations. In the picture of 'Lord Cholmondeley and his Family,'[1] painted in 1732 before the days of Hogarth's fame, but when he had come to the full enjoyment of his powers, there is a smiling intimacy, which is intensely pleasing. The scene is a richly furnished apartment, with an alcove or gallery devoted to the display of the owner's pictures, the details of which are tantalisingly difficult to make out. Attention is immediately attracted to the two boys, who are not worked into the main composition, but have the right side of the picture to themselves. They are engaged in building a house or tower by piling a number of folio volumes on a chair. One boy mischievously gives the books a kick, as if to overthrow the structure, while the other looks on, undecided whether to protect the pile or to watch the result of his brother's audacity, which will soon spoil the serenity of the older folk, so very conspicuously sitting for their portraits. The young man standing behind Lord Cholmondeley has been identified as the peer's brother. If it were not for

[1] The picture, which is in the possession of the Marquess of Cholmondeley, was shown at the exhibition of Conversation Pieces in 1930 and at Paris in 1938.

HOGARTH. LORD CHOLMONDELEY AND HIS FAMILY
From the painting in the possession of the Marquess of Cholmondeley

his elegant attire, he might be thought of as the boys' governor or tutor; at any rate, he is the only one who gives them any attention.

Over the head of Lady Cholmondeley are two Cupids, like the similar figures in the 'Beckingham Wedding,' who draw aside a curtain which protects the library shelves. These cherubs, obviously intended to add a touch of fancy to the scene, are pleasantly decorative, form an amusing contrast to two real boys, and balance the composition.

The perfect mingling of an ethical purpose with the conventions of the conversation-piece is seen in a picture painted for Lord Charlemont in 1759,[1] which unites a realistic scene in high life with a sermon against gaming. A handsome officer who has been playing at cards with a fashionable young matron has won all her money and jewels, which he now offers in exchange for her virtue. When first exhibited in 1761 by the Society of Artists, Hogarth entitled the picture, 'Picquet or Virtue in Danger'; but it is invariably referred to as the 'Lady's Last Stake.' It was probably suggested by the dramatic situation at the opening of the second scene of the fifth act of Cibber's comedy of the same title (1708), where Lord George Wronglove and Lady Gentle are discovered rising from play, at which the lady has just lost a thousand pounds.[2] Hogarth has of course modernised the costumes, and introduced into his picture many characteristic details: it is thus described in the catalogue of Hogarth's paintings and sketches exhibited in the British Gallery in 1814:[3]

A young married lady is exhibited, who has lost her property to a handsome young officer of her own age. A letter from her husband, enclosing her a note of 500*l*, is on the ground: this, together with her watch, the miniature of her husband, and all her jewels, appears to be among the losses of the night. The officer is represented in the act of

---

[1] *Hogarth Illustrated*, vol. III, pp. 196 ff.

[2] Lord George: 'These bills, Madam, now are yours again. But why this hard, unkind concern? Be just at least, and don't in these reluctant tears, drown all the humble hopes that Fortune has bequeathed to me.'

Dobson pointed out Hogarth's possible use of an essay by Edward Moore in *The World* for December 11, 1755 (no. 154), which contains an anecdote of 'one of the finest women about St. James's,' who loses various parts of her attire at a game of picquet, but is saved from disgrace by a turn of Fortune. The author's use of the phrase, 'last stake,' seems to indicate that he had Cibber's play consciously or unconsciously in mind.

[3] Nichols and Steevens, *Supplementary Volume to the Works of Hogarth*, 1817, pp. 170–71.

HOGARTH. THE LADY'S LAST STAKE

From the painting in the possession of J. P. Morgan, Esq.

returning his gains, with the hope of exchanging them for a softer acquisition, and a more delicate plunder. The artist has caught his heroine
during the moment of hesitation and struggle with herself. On the
chimney-piece is a watch-case, and Cupid representing a figure of Time
over it; with this motto, '*Nunc*.' This, together with the horns of the
moon, requires no explanation. The candles nearly burnt out, and the
cards partly scattered on the ground and thrown into the fire, are indications of the scene that has passed.

It was asserted more than once by Dr. Johnson's vivacious
friend, Hester Thrale Piozzi, that, when a girl, she had posed for
the figure of the lady. In a letter to Sir James Fellowes, dated
October 30th, 1815, she told a long and circumstantial story
which, though hardly acceptable in all details, it is impossible to
reject. Miss Balderston, editor of *Thraliana*, regards the story as
reliable in outline, and points out that Mrs. Piozzi had no need to
invent compliments to herself. The most important part of the
story told to Sir James is the following:

The next time we went to Leicester Fields, Mr. Hogarth was painting, and bid me sit to him. 'And now look here,' said he, 'I am doing
this for you. You are not fourteen years old yet, I think, but you will be
twenty-four, and this portrait will then be like you. 'Tis the lady's last
stake; see how she hesitates between her money and her honour. Take
you care; I see an ardour for play in your eyes and your heart; don't indulge it. I shall give you this picture as a warning, because I love you
now, you are so good a girl.' In a fortnight's time after that visit we went
out of town. He died somewhat suddenly, I believe, and I never saw
my poor portrait again; till, going to Fonthill many, many years after-
ward, I met it there, and Mr. Piozzi observed the likeness.[1]

The picture sold to Lord Charlemont is now in the collection
of Mr. J. P. Morgan. Because of the great success of the piece, no
doubt, Hogarth painted a replica — the picture afterwards seen
by Mrs. Piozzi at Fonthill — now in the possession of the Duke of
Richmond and Gordon, at Goodwood, Sussex.[2] Both are authen-

---

[1] Hayward, *Autobiography*, etc., vol. II, p. 309. In the *Anecdotes of Johnson* (1786),
she says only, 'His [Hogarth's] discourse commonly ended in an ethical dissertation, and
a serious charge to me, never to forget his picture of the Lady's Last Stake.'

[2] The Charlemont picture was shown by Messrs. Knoedler at their gallery, in November, 1935; the Duke of Richmond's picture was in the exhibition of English Conversation Pieces, held in London in the spring of 1930. See the catalogue by Dr. G. C.
Williamson, London, Batsford, 1931.

tic, but neither supplies all the details mentioned in the catalogue description quoted above.

These conversation-pieces, striking and amusing though they be, did not satisfy Hogarth's ambition. Such canvases were delivered to those who had commissioned them, without being exhibited, and shut up in town or country houses, to be seen no more; whereas the painter felt the impulse within him to address his work to the public — to a large and applauding audience. Of his ability to catch and hold public attention he could have had no doubt. There was a growing interest in pictures, and a willingness to enjoy them at second hand by looking at prints; but it was hardly possible to acquire prints of conversation-pieces which had been privately commissioned. Even if prints were made, few could be sold, since their appeal would be merely local and private. Moreover, many of the persons represented would probably not have consented to let prints be taken of such intimate scenes, and publicly sold in shops. Hogarth therefore chose another means of appeal which enabled him at once to express his artistic purpose and to gain a livelihood. He refused to capitulate and become a mere manufacturer of stylish portraits, though he could paint admirable likenesses when no flattery or amelioration was demanded of him.[1]

His greatest pleasure as a painter was to represent human beings in groups. His instinct was for dramatic scenes. If his pictures gave spectators something to talk about, all the better; if they were so vivid as to influence the lives and opinions of men, better still; for thus the painter was shown to be no slave of the wealthy classes, but an independent commentator on the daily lives of men, like his friend Fielding. The desire to make painting a more vital concern to his countrymen accounts for all that he stood for — the moral lessons that he conveyed, his dogmatic assertions about the nature of beauty, his opposition to the founding of a Royal Academy, his ridicule of Continental standards and of the Italian tradition, his hostility, in short, to everything that obstructed the free expression of the painter's individuality.

Such a man will certainly be addicted to experiments, and it is

[1] Cf. Ireland, vol. III, pp. 32 ff.

with experiments, even when not very successful, that we are here concerned. It has already been said that there is a peculiar interest in pictures painted in defiance of the current styles and the public demand; and no one has ever painted more defiantly than Hogarth in his attempt to get his pictures before the eyes and attention of men. Though not a specially religious man, he even tried his hand at ecclesiastical and Biblical subjects,[1] because the walls of hospitals and other charitable institutions might be decorated by painters if only subjects could be found suitable to the surroundings, and directors be persuaded to permit the walls to glow with colour and to record a story. It is customary to deplore the existence of Hogarth's religious paintings, but, however defective in sentiment they may be, they abound in characteristic details which none but he would have dared to introduce into such pictures.

Such are the 'frescoes' in St. Bartholomew's Hospital, Smithfield, which, painted specially for the grand staircase, were presented by the artist, who, born in the parish, had been interested in this charity from his youth up. These frescoes, painted on canvas, of course, not on the plaster of the walls, have lately been cleaned, and, though ill lighted, may be inspected by the curious. They depict 'The Good Samaritan' and 'Christ at the Pool of Bethesda,' the former indicative of the hospital's function in cases of accident, the latter, in cases of illness. They are, in a sense, conversation-pieces in Palestinian or Biblical terms, and like much of Hogarth's work, humanitarian in appeal, though they were not designed for the amusement of the patients, but as decorations to touch the hearts of friends and visitors. In recognition of his philanthropic purpose and his devotion to St. Bartholomew's, Hogarth was made a life-governor of the foundation.

The less important of the pair is the Samaritan. He is pouring

[1] In 1756 he painted a large triptych for the high altar of the church of St. Mary Redcliffe, Bristol. The pictures, representing the Resurrection and Ascension, are not without interest; but since their removal from the church the canvases have been kept rolled up in the vault of the Royal West of England Academy.

This work had been preceded, eight years before, by a commission from the Benchers of Lincoln's Inn. Hogarth chose for his subject 'St. Paul before Felix,' and the picture, though it has had few admirers, still hangs in the Old Hall. Hogarth burlesqued his own painting in the subscription-ticket issued when the picture was first shown.

HOGARTH.   THE GOOD SAMARITAN

HOGARTH.   THE POOL OF BETHESDA

From the paintings in St. Bartholomew's Hospital, London

oil into the traveller's wounds, as the priest and the Levite disappear into the distance. His horse is a deplorable object, like nothing equine, but the dog licking his own sores — for the faithful cur, too, has been hurt by the highwaymen — is exceedingly Hogarthian. The wounded man affords the artist an opportunity to paint the nude. So does the 'Pool of Bethesda.' In that crowded scene there are two figures almost completely nude, the paralytic who is talking with the Saviour, and a female, evidently a lady of high birth, with an attendant standing by, ready to assist her into the water at the moment of its 'troubling' by the angel. The figures of Christ and the seraph above the Pool are so painfully bad that one turns for relief to look at the sick folk. For these Hogarth found his models among the patients in the hospital: cancer, palsy, and rickets are among the diseases which a physician recognises at once, and wounded and crippled figures abound. But the most Hogarthian touch of all is the introduction of two Cockney women, who look with angry and jealous surprise at the Saviour's miraculous healing of the paralytic, which is, plainly, not according to the rules. I remember nothing more typical of the painter's ironical humour than this comment on human pettiness.

Hogarth gave other paintings to the hospital, but it would be an error to devote to these an attention which may more profitably be expended on the other London charity which engaged his affections and which moved him to paint not only one of his amusing Biblical scenes, but also his masterpiece in portraiture. His devotion to the Foundling Hospital and its great benefactor, Captain Coram, forms the pleasantest chapter in his biography.

The Foundling Hospital, situated at that time off Guilford Street, near Brunswick Square,[1] for the maintenance and education of exposed and deserted children, was opened as a result of the exertions, extended over seventeen years, of Thomas Coram, a man of tireless energy, whose every ambition and thought centered in this charitable enterprise. 'On March 25, 1740/41,' say the historians of the Hospital,[2] 'a shield that had been specially

---

[1] At first in Hatton Garden.

[2] R. H. Nichols and F. A. Wray, *History of the Foundling Hospital*, London, 1935, p. 36.

designed by Hogarth . . . was set up over the door of the premises
. . . the gates were opened, and the Foundling Hospital came into
being.' One hundred and thirty-six children were admitted during the first year.

The relation which Hogarth contrived to establish between
this asylum and the associated painters of England was of almost
equal service to both. The hospital actually became a kind of art-
gallery, and numbered among its benefactors Reynolds, Gainsborough, Hayman, and Wilson. A series of circular paintings
representing the principal charitable institutions of London was
planned and completed, and is still among its valued possessions.
Of these the picture of the Foundling Hospital itself and that of
the great St. George's, Westminster, were presented by Wilson in
1746, and that of the Charterhouse — a lovely example of his
early work — by Thomas Gainsborough two years earlier.

Hogarth was largely if not entirely responsible for this link between
charity and art. The celebrated artist was a close friend and supporter
of Captain Coram, and was not only an original member of the Foundation under the Charter, under the denomination of 'a Governor and
Guardian,' but a zealous and active member of its Courts and General
Committee.[1]

Hogarth also designed the arms of the foundation, the original
drawing of which is preserved in its archives. On the shield is a
naked baby, with its right hand raised as if in supplication; on the
other side are allegorical figures of Britannia and of Nature, whose
nude torso is covered with breasts,[2] as if to represent fertility. The
crest is a lamb, and the motto the single word, 'Help.' He drew
also the design or head-piece for the subscription-roll, which represents the children at the door of the hospital, carrying various
implements which denote the practical education they receive.
Captain Coram, bearing the famous charter of the foundation,
accompanies a beadle who is bringing in a baby just surrendered
by a weeping but poverty-stricken mother. In the lower left-

---

[1] Nichols and Wray, p. 249.

[2] Cf. Hogarth's well-known print, 'Boys peeping at Nature,' a strange conception,
of which he twice made use, once in the subscription-ticket for the 'Harlot's Progress,'
1731, and again in that for the engraving of 'Moses brought to Pharaoh's Daughter,'
1752.

HOGARTH.   SKETCH FOR THE COAT OF ARMS OF THE
FOUNDLING HOSPITAL

HOGARTH.   DESIGN FOR THE SUBSCRIPTION-ROLL OF THE
FOUNDLING HOSPITAL

From Nichols and Wray's *History of the Foundling Hospital*, reproduced here
by permission of the Governors of the Foundling Hospital, London.

hand corner is an exposed infant; and, in the middle distance, what I take to be a woman in the act of abandoning her unwelcome offspring in a place where it will be found and rescued by Coram. 'In the other corner are three boys coming out of the door with the King's Arms over it, with emblems of their future employ-ments — one of them handles a plummet, a second holds a trowel, while a third, whose mother is fondly pressing him to her bosom, has in his hand a card for combing wool.' [1]

Hogarth, as I have said, presented to the hospital two large pictures, a portrait and a Biblical subject. It is convenient to speak first of the latter. The painters associated with the Found-ling seem, in certain instances, to have agreed with one another respecting the scenes to be illustrated by them; thus Hayman took the 'Finding of Moses among the Bulrushes,' and Hogarth that of 'Moses brought before Pharaoh's Daughter,' illustrating the verse, 'And the child grew and she brought him unto Pharaoh's daughter, and he became her son, and she called his name Moses.'

In this picture the boy, who is apparently less than three years old, clings to the skirts of his nurse, and gazes with curiosity and a certain disfavour upon his new mother. Egypt is indicated by the architecture in the background, particularly by a pyramid; and there is a small crocodile or alligator that emerges, surprisingly, from under the Princess's seat, an Egyptian and zoölogical detail certain to interest the orphans. Moreover, the picture conveys a lesson hardly to be missed by the dullest of the children; for here is the greatest of all foundlings, Moses, the beloved of God, who became the leader of his people and the law-giver of the human race.

But the incident which none but Hogarth would have invented is in the upper right-hand corner, where an Ethiopian is whisper-ing slyly to a lady-in-waiting. His leer seems to announce that the Princess has her own very private reason for adopting the little boy. This odd touch, noticed in the eighteenth century, may possibly be a glance at the fact that most of the children in the hospital were of illegitimate birth. To modern taste, this seems somewhat gratuitous.

[1] Nichols and Wray, pp. 249, 279.

This easel-picture has few admirers. We do not willingly tolerate serious subject-pictures from a painter habitually regarded as a great comic dramatist. In this respect Hogarth has been his own worst enemy, as was our American humourist who ventured to write a life of Joan of Arc. This is certainly the best of the Biblical paintings, and, like his later picture of 'Sigismunda weeping over the Urn containing the Heart of Guiscardo,'[1] might have been more highly esteemed, had it come from another hand.

Hogarth is at his greatest when his magnanimity unites with and dominates, but does not destroy, his comic power. Such a union is seen in the great portrait of Captain Coram, which the painter presented to the hospital, and which is still its proudest possession. Painted in 1740, when the institution was opened, it represents the Founder, now over seventy years old, in the hour of his triumph. Though in the hard, clear, literal style of all Hogarth's finished portraits, it contains, nevertheless, as many accessory details[2] as though it had been painted by Reynolds. The old man sits at a table on which lies the royal charter, obtained by his efforts, and holds in his hand the great seal which Hogarth had designed. A globe at his feet is so turned as to show the Atlantic Ocean and the continent of North America, for Coram had sojourned for a time — no doubt to his great educational advantage — in Boston, and later in Taunton. Since in both places he had followed his trade of ship-builder, the open casement affords a glimpse of ships at sea. The beaming countenance of the philanthropist reveals his depth and warmth of heart; yet the picture is without a trace of sentimentality. Here is no merely 'good-natured man,' the prey of ill-regulated emotions, but a sane,

---

[1] At the close of his career he put forth all his power upon this canvas, and defiantly challenged comparison with the Italian School. The picture is not without merit; but the artist's contemporaries, led by John Wilkes, a son of Belial, shrieked with laughter over the poor painter's attempt to be serious. The picture is at present (1938) shown at the Tate Gallery. But posterity has refused to pay it more honour than did its eighteenth century critics.

[2] Again, in the portrait of Mary Evans in the Frick Collection, he introduced not only a dog, but a globe, a scroll, two small busts, and the cords and tassels of the conventional curtain. There are ecclesiastical embellishments in the portrait of Bishop Hoadley in the Tate Gallery, and all manner of detail in the picture of the Graham Children in the National Gallery.

HOGARTH.   MOSES BROUGHT TO PHARAOH'S DAUGHTER

From the painting in the Foundling Hospital, London, reproduced here by permission of
the Governors of the hospital

patient, and practical man, determined, even-tempered, and invincible. Hogarth himself delighted in this portrait, and called it his best — the one, he writes,[1] 'which I painted with most pleasure, and in which I particularly wished to excel,' and adds, ingenuously, that it is 'generally thought the best portrait in the place, notwithstanding the first painters in the kingdom exerted all their talents to vie with it.'

I am inclined to think that the portrait of Coram reveals more of Hogarth's essential benevolence and more of his capacity for communicating and promoting good will among men than all his moral engravings. What more effective way of encouraging goodness of heart than by depicting its manifestation in such a man as Coram, and who can doubt that the respect for magnanimity thus created will result in an emulation of it? Here indeed is the humanitarian purpose operating in harmony with the artistic impulse.

Hogarth's philanthropy was of course expressed in the great series of narrative engravings upon which his fame has largely reposed, and in which he himself avowed that he had a moral purpose. But there is a vital difference between such a purpose and the humanitarian temper; in the former we detect, and often resent, a tendency to judge, to correct, and to chasten the erring; whereas in the latter the ruling motive is to succour and to heal. With the moral aspect of Hogarth's work the weary and puzzled world of to-day has no deep sympathy. It is not from Tom Careless and Moll Hackabout that we shall discover the way out of the wilderness in which we find ourselves; yet, after all concessions have been made, there is something in the engravings to fascinate us still. What is it in these rather crude pictures that arrests and holds us? The power of the Comic Muse? That, no doubt, but there is more than humour in them. In the two famous Progresses, for example, there is surely nothing funny in the final scenes, which disclose in pitiless detail scenes of insanity, disease, and death, and attain in truth all the power of tragedy except its sublimity. Pity and terror are there in full measure, and pity and terror transcend the comic stage. No, we cannot dispense with the moral lessons,

[1] Ireland, vol. III, p. 48.

HOGARTH.   CAPTAIN CORAM

From an engraving of the portrait in the Foundling Hospital, London, reproduced
here by permission of the Governors of the hospital

shriek hilariously over the comic scenes, and pretend to have gone to the heart of the matter. Charles Lamb, over a century ago, in pointing out the true significance of Hogarth, insisted on the presence in his work of an element of tenderness. I prefer to call it *sensitivity*, if the word is permissible, a sensibility, that is, which in this case conceals itself under a brusque exterior. It is hidden by his pugnacity, by his tendency to dogmatise and argue, and by his habit of hurling his common sense as a battering ram against the walls of privilege and pretense.

From one series of engravings Lamb shrank in dismay, as an unspeakable aberration of the artist's hardly to be pardoned — the 'Four Stages of Cruelty' (1751), a group of pictures showing the progress of that vice from its first stage in the torture of animals to its culmination in mutilation and murder. Although one instinctively shares Lamb's abhorrence of these plates, it is impossible to deny that in the present instance they form a climax, albeit disagreeable, to the theme. Hogarth issued an impression on common paper, which was put on sale at a shilling the set, so that they might be within reach of boys of the lower classes, whose hearts he hoped to touch. To us the pictures seem less like an appeal than a shriek of indignant horror; but of the motive behind them there can be no doubt. The man who drew these dreadful scenes was obviously driving himself to the minute inspection of a current vice, as a physician investigates the cause and progress of a disease.

The 'Four Stages' must not be dismissed as indications of the artist's declining powers, since the plates belong to the same general period as the great 'March to Finchley' (1750), and precede the 'Election' series (1755); moreover they are but the focus of a score of similar details in preceding pictures. In the famous picture of 'Strolling Actresses dressing in a Barn' (1738), two old women are depicted as lacerating the tail of a cat, and grinning at the animal's contortions — a passage which most admirers of that amazing plate prefer to ignore. The same desire to expose a vice and the same determination to rouse a sluggish world account for the painter's exposure in the 'Harlot's Progress' of the overseer's cruelty at Bridewell, and the careful record of the horrors of the madhouse in the 'Rake's Progress.'

I have used the word *humanitarian* in its narrower sense as synonymous with philanthropic; but in its deeper and truer significance as indicative of that magnanimity which finds a sufficient inspiration in the men and manners of one's own day, it is also applicable to Hogarth, as it is to his friend Fielding. His finest portrait, now also his best-known picture, the 'Shrimp Girl' in the national collection, reveals that temper no less fully than does the 'Captain Coram' at the Foundling, since she makes us find our own kind likable and jolly, and renders us the happier for it. She radiates health, good-will, young beauty and laughter, as Coram typifies aged benevolence and faith in human values. All this is the outcome of the clear vision of the artist and the ruthless hand of the craftsman, operating in ardent response to a delight in the drama of existence, which is Hogarth's most conspicuous endowment.

III

REYNOLDS: ROMANTIC TENDENCIES

IT seems paradoxical to speak of the 'romanticism' of so sedate and self-controlled a man as Reynolds. A most prolific painter, he sat at his easel all day, and never brooded, or frittered away his time awaiting inspiration. He took up his palette and brushes, and set to work. There was sufficient inspiration in that. His appointment-book shows that on the day when he was knighted, he had a sitter at eleven o'clock in the morning, went to court for the ceremony at half-past twelve, and then returned to his studio for an appointment at two in the afternoon. He had no trace of what has since been called temperament, no fits of melancholy, and no Bohemian tastes. He made several journeys to the Continent, but can hardly be described as a traveller. At least travel was not necessary to stimulate his activity; there was stimulus enough in London itself. He lived contentedly in Leicester Fields, an urbane and quiet gentleman, whom Goldsmith praised as 'bland' and Johnson as 'inoffensive.' A fashionable painter must be all things to all men, and suffer fools gladly. At his worst, Reynolds was thought merely cold and unconcerned. 'His heart was too frigid,' wrote Mrs. Piozzi, 'his pencil too warm.'

How, then, shall such a man be called romantic? Yet during the last two decades of his career, the current of his interests set strongly towards imaginative and even melodramatic subjects. Wealthy and famous, he was free to paint as he pleased, and his pleasure proved to be in 'old, unhappy, far-off things.' In the very 'warmth' of his style, in his uncompromising determination to idealise his sitter, and, in his own words, to give 'grace and dignity to the human figure,'[1] there are revealed an ambition to be more than a mere manufacturer of likenesses, and a wish to escape from the commonplace fashionable life of London. No nobler defence of such a desire can be found than his words at the end of his ninth Discourse:

[1] *Discourse* I.

The art which we profess has beauty for its object; this it is our business to discover and to express; the beauty of which we are in quest is general and intellectual; it is an idea that subsists only in the mind; the sight never beheld it, nor has the hand expressed it: it is an idea residing in the breast of the artist, which he is always labouring to impart, and which he dies at last without imparting.

Here is that abiding faith in the unattainable —'quest' is Sir Joshua's word — which is never dissociated from the romantic mood, that interest in the far away and the long ago, that 'idea subsisting in the breast of the artist,' which must be expressed, as well as might be, through the conventions of the school to which he belonged and of which he was the official head and leader. The poetic spirit of the day was far-sighted, centrifugal, dissatisfied with the actual and the familiar. Gray and Ossian, Percy and Chatterton, Mason and Walpole had set readers to looking backward for beauty and for stimulus to the imagaintion. Reynolds, tremulously responsive to literary movements about him, is therefore not without indication of such interests if we have but the ingenuity to recognise them.

One evidence of this romantic quest is the delight which he took in painting children. No English painter can vie with him for a moment in his depiction of childhood, its activity, its changefulness, its wide-eyed wistfulness — as if looking out upon the world with a piercing inquiry — a trait which no earlier artist had recorded. There were, to be sure, sides of child-life which Reynolds did not attempt to paint, its noise, dirt, and selfishness. Hogarth saw such facts, and grimly set them down in 'Noon' and 'Evening,' and the last two scenes of the 'Harlot's Progress.' Reynolds paints only 'nice children,' but contrives to show them as human, even though on their good behaviour. Like many another bachelor, he was fond of children, divined what was in their minds, and knew how to gain their confidence. Northcote, his follower and biographer, wrote,

Oh what grand rackets there used to be at Sir Joshua's when these children were with him. He used to romp and play with them, and talk to them in their own way.[1]

[1] *Life*, p. 78.

A picture which has recently attracted much favourable attention is that of the third Lord Grantham as a boy, with his two brothers, the Hon. Frederick and the Hon. Philip Robinson. It was shown in Amsterdam in 1936, and in London, at the Reynolds Exhibition, in 1937. It is a large canvas, with a good deal of space about the figures, and a pleasant landscape background, painted in the artist's sixty-fifth year (1788) and therefore in his latest manner, but it has as much vigour as if it had been produced thirty years before. I am not sure just what the boys are up to. Perhaps the two elder ones are supposed to be inciting their dogs to bark, and the youngest intervenes, while his brother seizes him by the hair to draw him away. But whatever the action may be, the boys seem to be entirely natural. It is, no doubt, a completely finished picture, but none the less the result of a momentary impression upon the artist's mind. It was exhibited at the Royal Academy in the year in which it was painted, and was engraved by Bartolozzi in 1791.

One of the painter's devices in dealing with children was to dress them in costume, and so turn the dullness of a 'sitting' into a lark. It amused them, and released his own fancy. In the portrait of the affectionate brothers he introduced no allegorical or histrionic fancies, as when he painted the familiar picture of Master Crewe (1775), dressed as King Henry VIII, with spaniels at his feet and a dagger at his side. In 1777, Lady Caroline Scott, a tiny being aged three, was brought to his studio one cold day, and he at once decided to paint her as she was, bundled up for warmth, with a wintry background of snow, diversified by a robin (somewhat disconsolate), and a contorted dog, which must not be too closely examined. But the picture is not remembered for its setting or accessories; the child is the centre and source of all the spectator's interest — a little girl whom Horace Walpole longed to seize and embrace. Though the title, 'Winter,' was given to the portrait when it was engraved by J. R. Smith (1779), Reynolds probably had no intention of painting his delightful little sitter as an allegorical presentment of one of the four seasons; but he certainly did not discourage the use of symbolic or sentimental titles by his various engravers. Such designations were useful as veiling the

REYNOLDS.   LORD GRANTHAM AND HIS BROTHERS
From the painting in the possession of Lady Desborough

identity of the sitters and advertising the picture. Fanciful titles
were even more commonly applied to engravings made from landscape-paintings.

The patient and wistful boy whom Reynolds painted in the
rôle of Mercury as Cutpurse,[1] a preposterously innocent patron of
footpads, is now unknown by name, though he has been known
for a century and a half in the engravings of him by Dean (1777).
He is also the model for 'Cupid as Link-Boy,' a youngster in jacket
and breeches, carrying a torch such as was used to light pedes-
trians through the streets at night—a highly appropriate employment for the young god of love.

The number of these romantic pictures of childhood is surprising.[2] There are Biblical subjects: Moses in the Bulrushes (a laughing child stretching arms of welcome to his discoverers), the Infant
Samuel, kneeling in prayer, the Infant Daniel, and the Infant
Baptist, preaching in the wilderness. A more pagan group includes the Infant Jupiter, the Infant Bacchus, Young Hannibal
(in armour), Robin Goodfellow, or Puck, a grinning urchin with
pointed ears, sitting on a huge mushroom, the Babes in the Wood,
a sleeping child, and a smiling gipsy boy. The son of the Duke of
Marlborough, aged five, is represented as a courtier in Van Dyck
attire, and his sister as a fortune-teller reading his palm.[3] An imaginary scene of babies in a studio, one at an easel, another in the
sitter's chair, is entitled 'The Infant Academy.'[4] The most preposterous of all, and certainly the most humorous, is that of the Infant
Johnson, of which I have spoken elsewhere. Its date and origin
are alike unknown. Reynolds seems to have amused himself with a
fancy as comic in nature as it was interpretative of his burly friend.
It is a reasonable inference that Samuel Johnson, who considered
Reynolds the most inoffensive of men, was kept in ignorance of its
existence.

The fancy-pictures of little girls are even better known than
those of boys. There is 'Muscipula,' a mouselike cottage-child

[1] In Lord Faringdon's collection.
[2] A partial list may be found in F. G. Stephens's *English Children as painted by Sir
Joshua Reynolds*, London, 1867; and in Northcote's *Life of Reynolds*, 1813.
[3] At San Marino.
[4] At Ken Wood. The original rough sketch is in my possession.

REYNOLDS. LADY CAROLINE SCOTT AS 'WINTER'

From the painting in the possession of the Duke of Buccleuch

looking at a mouse in a trap, 'Felina,' with a kitten, 'Lesbia,' with a dead sparrow, 'Robinetta,' with a bird on her shoulder, 'Collina' on a hill-top; and 'Dolores,' sitting with folded hands and undried tears, in patient sorrow. There are the five angel-heads of little Isabella Gordon, forming one picture; and Theophila Gwatkin, sitting on the ground, with clasped hands, a picture engraved as 'The Age of Innocence.' The last two pictures, in the National Gallery, have been cheapened by all manner of reproductions, and even used for the decoration of lamp-shades. To modern taste they are cloyingly sweet; but to the student of the eighteenth century that sweetness is precisely the significant thing about them. Their sentimentality does not exceed that of the contemporary painters in France — François Greuze, for example, whose 'Broken Pitcher,' 'L'Oiseau Mort,' 'L'Effroi,' 'Prière du Matin,' and a dozen other canvases are admirable illustrations of the fashionable sensibility of the day. Children, and their joys and sorrows, are of increasing importance in poetry till the sentiment culminates in Blake's *Songs of Innocence* (1789). Picture and poem alike mark the discontent with that sophistication which had been so prominent in the earlier half of the century and which is sometimes thought of, wrongly, as typical of its entire course.

Interest in childhood itself betrays the romantic preoccupation with the far away and the long ago; and closely related with it is interest in the child-man, the primitive being close to the heart of Nature, unspoiled by the western world — man as he had issued from the Creator's hand. Reynolds's interest in picturesque persons from distant lands will startle only those who think of him exclusively as Painter to the World of Fashion. As a matter of fact, he delighted to paint the exotic.

An odd example of this taste for 'primitivism' (as it is now pedantically termed) is his portrait of the Hon. Mrs. Tollemache as 'Miranda,' painted in 1773, and engraved by John Jones in 1785.[1] Caliban, with a load of sticks, occupies the lower right-hand corner. His face, seen in profile, under a stiff shock of unkempt hair, is marked by a vast moustache, sweeping across a

---

[1] The original painting is at Ken Wood; one of the engravings is in the New York Public Library.

REYNOLDS.   MERCURY AS CUTPURSE

From the picture in the possession of Lord Faringdon

grinning mouth, from which protrude tusklike teeth. His right hand, carefully indicated, is half talon, and half paw. But Reynolds, for all his sentiment, missed the poetic strain so prominent in Shakespeare's child-man. Prospero's austere countenance is visible among the trees, and the shipwreck is shown in the distance. But the picture, which has faded sadly, is now hardly in a state to be reproduced.

There were occasionally opportunities to paint persons from the near East, or even genuine Orientals. In the so-called portrait of Lord Clive and his Family, at Bridgewater House (painted in the decade of the 'sixties), there is a Hindoo nurse or *ayah* in the centre of the group, the most conspicuously attractive feature of the picture. There is a pleasant portrait of Mrs. George Baldwin, the Greek wife of the English consul at Smyrna, dressed in Turkish costume, seated cross-legged on a divan.[1] She has almond-shaped eyes, and wears a turban on her unpowdered hair. This picture, painted in 1782, was praised for its eastern tone.

In Wang-y-Tong, a Chinese boy brought to England by Captain Blake, Reynolds had a far eastern sitter. The youth had been taken under the protection of Lord Sackville (who appears to have commissioned the portrait), and was put to school at Seven Oaks.[2] The picture, over four feet in height, finished, apparently, in 1776, is still in the possession of the Sackville family.

Wang-y-Tong, a pleasant-looking boy some fourteen or fifteen years old, one would say, is in full Chinese garb, sitting cross-legged on a low settee — a typical bit of eighteenth century Chinoiserie — with an odd conical cap on his head, a pair of square-toed red slippers on his feet, and a Chinese fan in hand. One can but wonder what was the future life of Wang-y-Tong.

---

[1] Mrs. Baldwin was acquainted with Fanny Burney (see *Diary of Mme. d'Arblay*, vol. II, pp. 70, 74). Miss Balderston has called my attention to the following passage in *Thraliana*, for April 13th, 1782:

'[I] hope to obtain some favours from the new Ministry for my pretty Greca: could her Husband *but* gain the Embassy! Oh I should not sleep for Pleasure. This pretty Greek as we call her, was born at Smyrna, & ran away with a Man whose Family had been some of Mr. Thrale's best Friends in the Borough: between Gratitude to *him*, and delight in her, for artlessness & Beauty, I have been led to interest myself no little towards protecting her.'

[2] See *Knole and the Sackvilles*, by V. Sackville-West, London, 1922.

REYNOLDS.   WANG-Y-TONG

From the painting in the possession of Lord Sackville

Was he returned to his home in China, with the western virus in his veins, or did he linger out his life in England, a somewhat exotic figure to the end?

For Omai, or Omiah, a young man from an island near Tahiti (or Otaheite), one has a warmer sentiment, since more is known about him.[1] He is encountered in the *Life of Johnson*, where his naïve and amusing, though dignified, presence fills one of the pleasantest of Boswell's pages; but his manners are there made to seem anything but uncivilised. Omai gave Sir Joshua his one contact with a savage, and the artist made the most of it. He painted him more than once. The picture here reproduced has recently come to light, is now in the Yale gallery, and seems to have been Reynolds's original sketch of Omai's head, a preliminary study for a more imposing picture. It shows a sitter, who, like Wang-y-Tong, was quite at ease in the presence of the artist. The ability to make his patrons happy was one of the painter's most amiable endowments, arising, I think, from a natural liking for human beings, which, if not deep, was at least easily stirred and renewed. There are portraits of Omai by other hands, notably one by Nathaniel Dance, which emphasises all the young man's Polynesian traits, and shows him holding his fan and his Otaheitan stool.[2] But Reynolds had no interest in these accessories. His was no document for the study of a South Sea Islander, but a painting of the Noble Savage; and therefore his heroic picture, known as the Castle Howard portrait,[2] shows Omai highly idealised and worthy to illustrate the theories of Rousseau or the later dreams of Chateaubriand. The turban which he wears gives him something of the dignity of an Arab, which is emphasised by the gesture of the

[1] I have given some account of Omai in *Nature's Simple Plan*, Princeton, 1922. He was brought to England by Captain Furneaux in the 'Adventure,' a sister-ship of Captain Cook's 'Resolution,' in 1774, at the end of Cook's second voyage to the South Seas. Two young savages consented to make the journey to England, but one died on the voyage, probably from exposure to the northern climates and the unnatural conditions on shipboard. Omai, however, reached England in safety, having apparently devised clothes for himself, of which he had been hitherto happily ignorant. Widespread interest was felt in this attractive savage, who proved to be as agreeable as Voltaire's Huron, because of his simple and easy manners. He dined with duchesses and the *literati*, and was presented at court, where he addressed George III as 'King Tosh.'

[2] Reproduced in *Nature's Simple Plan*.

REYNOLDS. OMAI

From the painting in the Gallery of Fine Arts, Yale University

right hand. The landscape is an early attempt by an English painter to imagine the scenery of the Society Islands.

Omai was, after a time, returned to his island home. He carried with him seeds and tools in order to encourage agriculture there; but he was never happy again, stirred the jealousy of his countrymen, and died soon after. William Cowper, in the first book of *The Task* (1785), speaks with indignation of the English treatment of this gentle savage, and draws a touching picture of Omai's future life in his distant home.[1]

Reynolds painted no red Indians as did Benjamin West (of the Academy); perhaps he had no opportunity to do so; perhaps he shrank from comparison with the Pennsylvanian, who was supposed to know all about redskins,[2] and had shown them in his famous history-piece, 'The Death of General Wolfe,' of which many replicas were made. Romney painted a portrait of Joseph Brant, or Thayandenagea, a Mohawk, who had been civilised by going to school in Connecticut (under Joseph Wheelock); and who, as a 'loyalist,' had been brought to London in 1776. The English painter, an incurable idealist, represented the Indian in full American regalia, with tomahawk and feathers, and shed upon him such nobility of mien that one seeing the portrait might blush to be a Caucasian.[3] It is significant of the romantic interest in primitive man that Romney's portrait of this American savage

[1] The dream is past; and thou hast found again
    Thy cocoas and bananas, palms and yams,
    And homestall thatched with leaves. But hast thou found
    Their former charms? . . .
    Thou climb'st the mountain top, with eager eye
    Exploring far and wide the watery waste
    For sight of ship from England. Every speck
    Seen in the dim horizon, turns thee pale
    With conflict of contending hopes and fears,
    But comes at last the dull and dusky eve,
    And sends thee to thy cabin, well prepared
    To dream all night of what the day denied.
                                        (Lines 639 ff.)

[2] He furnished the drawing for Goldsmith's *Animated Nature* (1774), representing the North American Indian (vol. II, p. 229). Another exotic picture by West is 'The Ambassador from Tunis, with his Attendants, as he appeared in England in 1781.' It is in the possession of M. René Brimo, of Paris. See the *Life and Studies of Benjamin West*, by John Galt, London, 1816.

[3] The picture is in the Ottawa gallery.

REYNOLDS.   RESIGNATION

From an engraving by James Watson, 1772

should be contemporary with Reynolds's portraits of the South Sea
Islander.

Another sitter who betrays Reynolds's interest in unsophisti-
cated folk is George White, an Irish workingman, said to have been
picked up in the streets. He is used again and again as a model
during the decade of the 'seventies, in the fancy-pictures of Reynolds and others, because of his unusual possession of a full beard
and moustache. He appears as a 'Captive,' a 'Captain of Ban-
ditti,' a 'Banished Lord,' and in other rôles, till one wearies of his
bushy countenance. He touches literature, however, in two pictures now forgotten — perhaps happily forgotten — but not without interest to the historians of romanticism.

The first of these, called 'Resignation,' represents a dying man,
sitting at a casement, gazing at the sunset. The original picture I
have not seen, but the engraving is more interesting than the
painting because the artist dedicated the print to Oliver Goldsmith, who had himself dedicated *The Deserted Village* to Sir Joshua
in 1770. In the inscription below the engraving the picture is
called an 'attempt to express a character in *The Deserted Village*,'
the retired man, who has quitted the world for the blessings of a
simpler life, and who

> Bends to the grave with unperceived decay,
> While Resignation gently slopes the way;
> And all his prospects brightening to the last,
> His heaven commences ere the world be past.

The age affords no better example of the reciprocity of poet and
painter.

Reynolds's interest in the romantic led him on one occasion to
paint a picture with a mediaeval theme, a scene from the *Inferno*,
of the most intensely tragic sort, which was later to engage the
attention of William Blake — 'Ugolino and his Sons dying in
Prison.' The canvas, painted in 1773, and engraved by Dixon in
1774, is in the Sackville collection at Knole. The extent of Reynolds's acquaintance with the story of Ugolino and the Archbishop
Ruggieri is unknown;[1] but it is probable that he knew nothing of

---

[1] Five lines from Dante (in Italian) were quoted in the catalogue of the Royal
Academy below the title of the picture when it was exhibited in 1773.

REYNOLDS.   UGOLINO

From an engraving by John Dean, 1774

the famous incident in the *Inferno* until it was called to his attention by others. It has been said that his picture was originally a simple portrait of White with a tragic expression; but that Burke and Gold-smith, on seeing it, exclaimed that it was worthy to stand for the head of Ugolino, and that Reynolds, having heard the story from his friends, thereupon enlarged his picture by adding the figures of the four sons grouped round their father. Such an anecdote has naturally injured the reputation of this ambitious picture. Many disliked it from the first; but it had its admirers, too. As late as 1833, Constable, in his lectures before the Royal Institution, used an engraving of it as an illustration of Sir Joshua's genius.[1] It should be regarded with indulgence, since, as I have remarked before, the eighteenth century portrait-painter had but few op-portunities to deal with a tragic or even a mediaeval subject.

Another specimen of the artist's grand manner is the 'Death of Dido,' of which two canvases are known, one in the Pennsylvania Museum, and another in the possession of the King of England. It shows Dido on the funeral pile, with her sister bending over in agonised discovery, while Iris appears in the clouds to release the soul of the dying queen. In the distance the galley of Aeneas puts out to sea. The picture, exhibited in 1781, is not without beauty, though the drawing did not pass uncensured. As a story-picture, it afforded the artist an opportunity to illustrate a romantic inci-dent from the *Aeneid*, and to depict a partially nude figure in the central position. The pose of the sister was used again in 'The Infancy of Hercules.'

A word must be said about Sir Joshua's grandiose designs for the great west window in New College, Oxford, the glass of which was executed by Thomas Jervais. The window, owing to a mis-taken theory of glass-staining, is to-day a disconsolate ruin in brown; but Reynolds's aims are known to us from certain of the original oil paintings for it, and the whole scheme from engravings. Although such a conventional subject as the Nativity can hardly be considered 'romantic,' the painter's treatment of it has some significant details. The central panel, a more or less conscious imitation of the famous 'Notte' of Correggio, shows the Christ-

[1] Leslie and Shirley's *Life of Constable*, p. 401.

REYNOLDS.   THE NATIVITY

From an engraving by G. and J. Facius, 1785

child in the manger, surrounded by young angels, and the light issuing from him illuminating the figure of the Virgin as she bends over him. George White, in robe and beard, is a supernumerary as St. Joseph in the background. The figure of the Madonna caused Reynolds the gravest concern, until he persuaded Mrs. Richard Brinsley Sheridan to pose for him. The original painting, exhibited in 1789, was burned at Belvoir Castle in 1816, and is therefore known only from the engraving of it. The seven allegorical figures of the theological and cardinal virtues, which fill the lower panels, portraits in Sir Joshua's most poetic manner, require no description here. 'Faith' and 'Hope' are still popular among his fancy-pictures; but Lady Dudley and Ward, who posed for 'Fortitude,' succeeded in being only a sort of Britannia, with shield and lion.

In 1785 the Empress of Russia honoured Reynolds with a commission for a large canvas, and so provided him with a superb opportunity to paint in the full romantic manner. He devised a vast symbolic piece to be called 'The Infancy of Hercules,' in flattering reference to the recent birth of that empire of which Catherine II was now the mistress. Walpole expresses regret that the painter did not select the subject of the youthful Peter the Great at work in the English shipyards:

What a fine contrast might have been drawn, as Peter threw off the imperial mantle, and prepared to put on trowzers, between the sullen indignation of his Russian attendants, and the joy of the English tars at seeing majesty adopt their garb! Peter learning navigation here in order to give a navy to his own country — how flattering to both nations! [1]

But Reynolds, who lacked Hogarth's knowledge and love of the common people, was too wise to attempt the representation of sailors and navvies.[2]

'The Infancy of Hercules' is still in the Hermitage, but in a ruined state, for the pigments have darkened and sunk into the

[1] Walpole, *Anecdotes of Painting in England . . . Volume the Fifth*, edited by Hilles and Daghlian, New Haven, 1937, p. 71.

[2] Northcote (*Life*, p. 330) says that Reynolds considered and rejected the subject of Queen Elizabeth's visit to Tilbury Camp in 1588. The appearance of Sheridan's *Critic* in 1779, with its immortal burlesque of this subject, may well have had something to do with his rejection of this perilous plan.

canvas, and it is no longer exhibited — a melancholy end for so ambitious an effort. Photographs of the picture as it is to-day are almost useless. A small repetition of it, in the vault of the Pennsylvania Museum, is in monochrome. The best impression of the picture as it left the easel of Sir Joshua is to be derived from the mezzotint by James Walker, dated January 1, 1792, which is here reproduced.

In the cradle, lying upon wolf-skins, the heroic infant crushes the serpents which have attacked him and his baby brother, cowering at his side. Alcmena, the mother, rushes into the room, accompanied by her attendants, in wild alarm, while Amphitryon, on the other side, gazes in astonishment at the miraculous courage of the child. In the clouds Juno witnesses the failure of her plan for destroying the heroic infant. To the left, prophesying the future splendour of Russian history, stands Tiresias, the blind seer, of whom Northcote[1] wrote:

I have understood that Sir Joshua told a friend that the attitude and expression of the prophet Tiresias, introduced in the groupe, were taken from those in which he had occasionally seen his deceased friend, Johnson.

It is, in other words, the pose used in the fine portrait of Johnson painted for his step-daughter, Lucy Porter, and engraved by Watson in 1770, which shows the sage without a wig and with his contorted hands in the same position as here. Tiresias may, therefore, be called another 'fancy' portrait of Johnson, with the surprising addition of a venerable beard.

The crowded scene is overloaded with allegorical meaning, and its sublimity is perilously near to the ridiculous. Horace Walpole found in it

the passions of a nursery, and the common expression of affrighted parents. . . . The parents would feel the same emotions if two large rats had got into the cradle.

However this may be, there is hardly a detail without adventitious interest. It is obviously another 'Nativity,' an unconscious parody of the central panel of the New College window, and includes even a Queen of Heaven, who inspects the scene from above. The

[1] *Life*, p. 331.

mother, her arms spread in convulsive terror, is reminiscent of Dido's sister, whose passion is similarly denoted. The central figure, another one of Reynolds's fancy pictures of childhood, is the best part of it, and was repeated again and again, omitting the cowardly Iphicles. Indeed, the athletic infant might be the child Johnson waked into frenzied activity.

There are other subject-pictures painted in the last period of Reynolds's activity: 'The Continence of Scipio' (1789); 'Cymon and Iphigenia,' sometimes called his last fancy subject, which is in Buckingham Palace, and therefore never seen by the public; 'The Death of Cardinal Beaufort,' an unhappy experiment in melodrama, showing the prelate at the moment of dissolution, with a demon in the shadows glaring at him. This last was painted as an illustration for Boydell's Shakespeare Gallery. Another Shakespearian subject is 'The Meeting of Macbeth and Banquo with the Witches'; but the heads of the weird sisters gave the artist some difficulty, as the number of preliminary rough sketches may indicate.

These 'fancy' or subject-pictures are not to be thought of as examples of a manner in any way peculiar to Reynolds. Benjamin West and others of the English School were already famous for them. Throughout the decade of the 'eighties there had been an increasing interest in 'historical' painting, which reached its climax in 1789 with the opening of John Boydell's Shakespeare Gallery in Pall Mall. The thirty-four oil paintings, representing subjects drawn from Shakespeare's plays, were the work of the most prominent artists in England, Romney, West, Opie, Fuseli, Northcote, Hamilton, Smirke, and Reynolds.[1] In the course of a twelvemonth the number of pictures exhibited was increased to sixty-six. In its first year the collection was enriched by seven 'miscellaneous' pictures (including Reynolds's great portrait of Lord Heathfield, the defender of Gibraltar, and Hogarth's 'Sigismunda'), all with some literary or historical interest. In 1790 this 'miscellaneous' group was enlarged to nineteen canvases

---

[1] Gainsborough had died in 1788; for his connexion with Boydell, see Whitley's *Thomas Gainsborough*, p. 269. Though he had painted a portrait of 'Garrick embracing a Bust of Shakespeare,' he was seldom interested in merely poetical painting.

REYNOLDS. THE INFANCY OF HERCULES
From an engraving by James Walker, 1792

(all subject-pieces), and 161 'drawings after the most capital pictures in England,' consisting of scenes prepared for engraving by Boydell, Earlom, and others. Among these were Gainsborough's 'Shepherd Boy,' and 'Girl and Pigs,' and Sir Joshua's 'Nativity,' from the New College window.

It was Boydell's intention to leave the whole collection to the nation, a generous ambition which was not to be realised. Indeed, his intention from the first had been to improve the lot of English artists. In the preface to his first catalogue, issued in 1789, he says:

> The Painter's labours will be perpetually under the public eye, and compared with those of his cotemporaries, while his other works, either locked up in the cabinets of the curious, or dispersed over the country in the houses of the different possessors, can comparatively contribute but little to his present fortune or his future fame.

Moreover, he hoped to direct the whole movement of English painting towards the historical style:

> The abilities of our best artists are chiefly employed in painting portraits of those who, in less than half a century, will be lost in oblivion,— while the noblest part of the Art, historical painting, is much neglected.

To correct this neglect was, he asserts, 'the principal cause of the present undertaking.' The views of Boydell, who had made a fortune out of the publication of prints by English engravers after pictures by English artists, were in harmony with the views of Sir Joshua Reynolds, as set forth in his *Discourses*. It was for the Shakespeare Gallery that Reynolds had painted the 'Death of Cardinal Beaufort' (an illustration for the *Second Part of King Henry VI*, 'See how the pangs of death do make him grin'), and 'Macbeth, Hecate, and the Witches.' His 'Robin Goodfellow,' or 'Puck,' was at one time intended for the Gallery. Romney's subjects: 'Cassandra Raving,' 'Prospero and Miranda,' and an allegorical piece, 'The Infant Shakespeare nursed by Tragedy and Comedy' (a subject suggested by Gray's *Progress of Poesy*), provided him with an opportunity to paint his favourite model, Emma Hart, afterwards Lady Hamilton.[1]

---

[1] Another phase of this interest in subject-painting is seen in Gainsborough's genrepieces, in Morland's scenes from fashionable life, and in the vast historical canvases of West and Copley.

All this time Reynolds continued to be active as a portrait-painter, showing no obvious decline in his power of producing a likeness or interpreting a character. He was in no sense at war with himself or the victim of divided aims. Although he never won popularity as a painter of subject-pictures, and received few commissions for them, there can be no doubt that his chief desire was to distinguish himself in that grand manner.

There has recently come to light a scrap-book containing some fifty rough sketches by Sir Joshua.[1] It is a strange volume, extending from the student-days in Italy to the final stage of his career; but the most significant thing about the drawings, considered as a collection, is that they have been arranged and numbered by the artist himself, and there must therefore be some relation among them. About a quarter seem to be studies or hasty notes of pictures seen in Italy; half the remainder are preliminary jottings later to be used in devising grand portraits (such, for example, as the Devonshire Family); and the rest seem to be related in some way to the subject of this paper, since they contain, among other hints, the first sketch for the 'Infant Academy,' the 'Nativity,' and two versions of a 'Meeting of Macbeth and Banquo with the Witches.' Just why these particular sketches, and not others which would seem naturally to belong with them, should have been classified together only Sir Joshua himself could say. But they all reveal his abiding passion to express ideal beauty in human form. This it was which underlay all his work, which shed upon his typical portraits — even upon what Burke once, in speaking of Reynolds, called 'mere heads'— that grace and dignity always associated with his name.

---

[1] It is at present in my possession.

IV

GAINSBOROUGH: RETURN TO NATURE

WHEN Gainsborough made his oft-quoted remark about Reynolds, 'Damn him, how various he is,' he was glancing, we may suppose, at the peculiar skill by which his great rival ran the whole gamut of portrait-painting, from 'mere heads' to the most elaborate poetic and allegorical fantasies. Gainsborough himself had no such variety, but painted his sitters, commonly, in their habit as they lived. Yet, in a larger sense, he was far more various than Reynolds. He excelled in two distinct branches of the art, portraiture and landscape, and revealed an unequalled success in combining the two — that is, in adjusting the human figure to a background of natural scenery. Moreover, he had more comprehensive interests than any painter of his time, since he excelled in conversation-pieces, animal painting, seascapes, genre, and even still life. Such was *his* peculiar variety.

Gainsborough's personality was also more vivid and various than that of Sir Joshua. He was excitable, easily moved to wrath and as readily appeased, generous and friendly with all who loved music and animals and the open air; but oppressed exceedingly by pretentiousness. He had not Reynolds's gift of suffering fools gladly, much less of seeing anything picturesque in their ostentation. Although he painted at court, he was not a courtly person, but preferred to associate with musicians, simple folk, and, on occasion, with cottagers. The result in his portraits is obvious. His most engaging pictures are those of persons with whom he was intimate or at ease. His grand sitters seem a little glacial, for all the perfection of the painter's technique, as though a pane of glass were between them and the artist.

The methods of the two painters are sufficiently indicated by their respective treatment of Mrs. Siddons. Reynolds, who was to depict the actress as the Tragic Muse, in classic robes, and with attendant allegorical figures of Crime and Remorse, is said to have remarked, as he assisted the actress to her seat on the dais, 'Ascend

GAINSBOROUGH.   THE DUKE AND DUCHESS OF CUMBERLAND

From the painting in Windsor Castle

GAINSBOROUGH.   LADIES WALKING IN THE MALL

From the painting in the Frick Collection

your undisputed throne'; and, when the portrait was finished, signed his name along the edge of her robe, in order to send his name 'down to posterity on the hem of her garment.' His astuteness as a courtier served him as a painter, and elicited that majestic dignity which characterises his representation of the great *tragédienne*. Gainsborough made no attempt, as he had no wish, to record the art of 'Queen Sarah'; but he was interested in the woman as she rustled into his studio in her blue and white silk dress. Her hat, muff and fur all delighted him, and he proceeded to paint her as though she were paying him a call. As an actress, she was one of those sitters with whom he could be informal; and, while drawing her striking profile, he is said to have remarked, 'Damn it, madam, there is no end to your nose.' The man who made such a remark was, clearly, no courtier, but a brusque and friendly being, concerned to rid his sitter of all sense of restraint. For a painter's studio is to the sitter a nerve-racking place, and the artist seems to be both judge and executioner. The victim is as self-conscious as he is likely to be at any time in his life; and self-consciousness is as a screen between him and the painter. When there is no communion between them the result is artificial, icily perfect, no doubt, but lacking the final grace of simplicity.

One way of overcoming the self-consciousness of a sitter is for the painter to get him out of the uncongenial atmosphere of the studio, and, if possible, into the open air. Gainsborough had from the first shown peculiar skill in representing his sitters as out of doors, and thus uniting portraiture with landscape. Moreover for him it must have enlivened the drudgery of mere 'face-painting.' In his youth he had painted a portrait of Mr. and Mrs. Andrews sitting in a wheat-field — a lovely picture, fresh as the dew of morning, in which Gainsborough's two major interests seem almost equally balanced; and at the close of his career his love of the scenery sometimes prevailed over his interest in the human beings, and resulted not so much in a portrait as in a picture of a garden or a park, animated by gallant men and gracious women.

So in the beautiful portrait of the Duke and Duchess of Cumberland, the royal personages are reduced almost to the level of figures enlivening a garden scene. Here are sweetness and distinction, without characterisation. We see, as it were, the Duke and Duchess passing a window through which we are privileged to look. And it is well that it should be so, for the Duke was dull and vicious, and his union with the Duchess unhappy. The scandal connected with them must have been known to Gainsborough, but the picture betrays no knowledge of it. Here, as at all times, he closes his eyes to vice, anger, and pain, and wears in their presence a mask of indifference or relapses into British impassiveness.

The tendency to prefer the scenery to the persons animating it reaches a climax in the famous canvas, 'Ladies walking in the Mall,' now in Miss Frick's gallery. It is a view of the central avenue of the Mall, near Gainsborough's residence, behind Carlton House. The identity of the fashionable ladies taking an afternoon stroll in the park is happily ignored. The rustling of the foliage is echoed, as it were, in the shimmer of the ladies' gowns, so that Horace Walpole wrote of the picture that it was 'all a-flutter, like a lady's fan.' It has the delicate grace of Lancret or Pater, and betrays the painter's ingenious escape from his studio to the greenest retreat which a Westminster life afforded him.

Gainsborough was somewhat less interested in poetry and men of letters than were other artists of the day. He had difficulty in making his work reflect the thoughts and emotions of other men. He could not be persuaded to contribute to Boydell's Shakespeare Gallery, though he is said to have tried — and failed — to produce for it an ideal portrait of the dramatist. He did, at the end of his career, accept a commission to contribute to Macklin's English Poets and two canvases resulted, both in the genre style, but neither particularly appropriate as an illustration. But it is not difficult to show that he responded to the same currents that influenced the poets, and it is not uncommon to find his work associated with theirs.

Thus the picture called 'Peasants at a Grave' could be associated by the publisher of the aquatint with poetry and styled 'A Country Churchyard.' This print, made after the death of Gainsborough in 1788, is dedicated to Sir Joshua Reynolds, who had eulogised the great landscapist in his fourteenth Discourse.

GAINSBOROUGH. MUSIDORA
From the painting in the National Gallery, London

Below the print are the first sixteen lines of Gray's Elegy; but the scene must not be thought of as Stoke Poges, for the church is in ruins, and the very gravestones are crumbling away. Over one of them bend a peasant and a cottage-girl, striving to decipher the inscription.[1] It is not only the rude forefathers of the hamlet who have passed away, but the hamlet itself and the church which was its centre — their very memory is not. Nevertheless the atmosphere of the picture is in perfect harmony with that which Gray and the Churchyard poets had popularised:

> Hark how the sacred calm that broods around
> Bids every fierce, tumultuous passion cease,
> In still small accents whispering from the ground
> A grateful earnest of eternal peace.

There are also poetic associations with the portrait of Musidora, who is the heroine of a pretty tale in James Thomson's 'Summer,' and the subject of scores of sentimental scenes painted by eighteenth century artists of lesser rank. On a hot summer afternoon, a maiden with this suggestive name sought out a retired spot on the banks of a stream, where she deemed it safe to remove her clothes and enjoy a cool plunge in the water. The poet, in the high strain of pastoral poetry, mentions how

> from the snowy leg
> And slender foot, the inverted silk she drew.

Meanwhile, unknown to her, her lover, Damon, having innocently followed from afar, was a felicitous spectator of the scene, a kind of happier Actaeon, for he eluded her notice altogether, so intent was she upon her sport. He retired in a rapture, and spent his emotion on a set of verses, which he hastily fastened to a tree, where Musidora might find them on emerging from the stream. In them he assured her that he would protect her retreat from intruders less scrupulous than himself.

However pompous the story may seem to-day, it provided a pleasant scene for painters in search of a 'fancy' theme, as well as

---

[1] See the frontispiece to this book. A variant of the scene, with a similar ruin, in which an old peasant is gazing at the epitaph and the lovers are reclining on the hillside, is reproduced by Mrs. Arthur Bell in *Thomas Gainsborough* (1897), opposite p. 14. It is said to be from an etching on pewter.

GAINSBOROUGH.   DIANA AND ACTAEON

From the painting in Windsor Castle

an opportunity to paint the nude. It used to be said that Gainsborough's model for Musidora was Emma Lyon, afterwards Lady Hamilton, but this attribution is now doubted. The picture has lost something of its former popularity, since it has grown somewhat dark.

The canvas reveals a significant restraint on the artist's part, since he omits altogether the rapturous glances of the lover hiding in the background. No doubt he feared to introduce a vulgar or comic note into the scene. But nude heroine and male intruder alike are found in another canvas quite different in kind, 'Diana and Actaeon,' a large picture, more than five feet by six, owned by the King, and seldom seen by the public.[1] It is perhaps Gainsborough's one experiment in the grand historic style, a kind of painting which he commonly eschewed, asserting that he had a 'cunning way of avoiding great subjects in painting.'

In 'Diana and Actaeon' there is a lovely wooded scene, with waterfall and pool in which the goddess and her nymphs have been bathing. Several nude figures are seen against the green and secluded background with which they are in perfect harmony of tone. But the picture, painted in Gainsborough's freest manner, remained unfinished; for Actaeon, the antlers already branching from his guilty forehead, is only roughly sketched in. It is significant that this should be the part of the picture left unfinished; for it would seem to be a feature of the legend on which Gainsborough did not care to ponder, a melodramatic incident, with no foundation in truth. If Damon, the innocent intruder, would have struck a false note in 'Musidora,' how much more offensive would be Actaeon, a figure at once unpleasant and unavoidable. Gainsborough took slight pleasure in the melodramatic or the ridiculous.[2] The omission of Actaeon's hunting dogs by a painter who generally delighted to have animals in his pictures is even more significant; for they would have to be shown as about to tear their master

---

[1] Bought by George IV, when Prince of Wales, from the artist's widow.

[2] 'The Donkey-Race,' a picture which I know only through a woodcut, is an exception to this statement. It is said to have been engraved by T. S. Engleheart.

In 'The Broken Egg,' a girl on her way to market lets fall an egg from her basket, as she gets a kiss from a peasant-boy. The painting, the exact date of which is not known, is in the Hartford Museum. It must belong to the same general period as 'Gipsies.'

GAINSBOROUGH.   THE GIPSIES

From an engraving by Wood, 1764

in pieces, and would thus heighten the horror which the painter wished to subordinate.

The atmosphere of remoteness and repose which, despite the subject, characterises this picture, has already been illustrated in the canvas later called 'A Country Churchyard' (painted in 1779), and is usually thought of as typical of Gainsborough's landscapes. It is, however, in striking contrast to his earlier scenes, where the visual images are sharply defined, and the figures animating the scene are painted with a Dutch literalness and simplicity. If we look back to 'The Rural Lovers' (engraved in 1760), there is no trace of sentiment in the two chief figures or in the scene itself, which can hardly be termed a background, since the human beings and the trees alike are only details in the landscape as a whole. Another similar picture, entitled 'Gipsies,' and engraved in 1764, is in the direct and downright manner later adopted by George Morland. There is nothing romantic in Gainsborough's depiction of these children of the woods, nor in that of the dog and the donkey which accompany them and share their existence. Over the camp-fire the evening meal is stewing in a soup-kettle, and a boy is sampling it with a large spoon which he will presently dip again into the savoury mess. He is watched by two older men smoking clay pipes, and by a pretty girl, holding the ass's bridle. This is the 'torpid life' of 'wild outcasts of society,' which Wordsworth was presently to define, not the free existence according to Nature, so easily idealised by poets.

These pictures are related to the genre-paintings of a later date by their atmosphere of peace and solitude. The violence and convulsion of Nature, which meant much to Turner and even to Wilson, never dominated the imagination of Gainsborough: storm and shipwreck, earthquake and conflagration are not found in his world. The subjects which gradually come to prevail are 'The Watering Place,' 'The Market Cart,' 'The Woodman's Return at close of day,' and 'The Cottage-Door,' of all of which there are variants and repetitions. 'The Cottage-Door' (1778; 75″ × 61″), now in the Huntington Gallery,[1] is typical of Gainsborough's

---

[1] There are repetitions in the National Museum, Washington, and in the collection of Mrs. Benjamin F. Jones, Jr., of Cincinnati.

GAINSBOROUGH.   THE COTTAGE-DOOR

From the painting in the Huntington Art Gallery, San Marino, California.

GAINSBOROUGH.   THE HOUSEMAID (THE COTTAGER'S DAUGHTER?)

Above, to the left, the artist's sketch; to the right, the oil sketch (life-size) in the National
Gallery; below, the cottager's daughter at the door, from a landscape in the
possession of Lord Tollemache

later manner. If I describe it as a 'return to Nature,' I wish to be understood as implying a return to things known and loved in the painter's passionate youth, from which the ungainly has disappeared or been transfigured by the selective powers of memory. Here is the full triumph of the romantic vision, the glowing recollection of a life simpler and more tender than any that he now could ever know. The little dwelling, tucked away under the trees, beside a waterfall, seems almost like a part of the natural scene. The life of the mother and children is passed on the breast of Nature, in poverty, no doubt, but in innocence, far from the folly and fever of the metropolis — shut away in safety.

The sentiment evoked by Gainsborough is admirably defined by Constable in his fourth lecture on landscape-painting: [1]

The landscape of Gainsborough is soothing, tender, and affecting. The stillness of noon, the depths of twilight, and the dews and pearls of the morning, are all to be found on the canvases of this most benevolent and kind-hearted man. On looking at them, we find tears in our eyes, and know not what brings them. The lonely haunts of the solitary shepherd, the return of the rustic with his bill and bundle of wood, the darksome lane or dell, the sweet little cottage girl at the spring with her pitcher, were the things he delighted to paint, and which he painted with exquisite refinement, yet not a refinement beyond nature.

There are several repetitions of 'The Cottage-Door.' In Lord Rutland's version, the cottager himself, returning with a load of faggots, is added, and there are three children, instead of six. As earlier in Gray's Elegy, and later, in 'The Cotter's Saturday Night,' the children are present to lisp their sire's return, and quiet evening ushers in the hour of rest.

If we isolate from this picture the group at the centre, we have a genre-scene of cottage-children at their supper, and a very attractive group it is, even without the trees and the waterfall. Gainsborough's later peasant-pictures spring out of such groups as this, which, in the earlier manner, had had no other function than to animate the scene. In the last period of his activity, large subjects sink into the landscape and become, as formerly, mere details; and, *vice versa*, details are taken out of landscape-paintings to form a genre-picture.

[1] Leslie and Shirley, p. 402.

Such a large picture later used as a detail in a landscape is a life-size portrait-sketch in the National Gallery, incorrectly entitled 'The Housemaid,' which should rather, I think, be called 'The Cottager's Daughter.' The earliest known form of this is a drawing six and a half inches high, found in a sketch-book of Gainsborough's [1] after his death, and there, as in the larger piece in the National Gallery, the scene is again the cottage-door. The small sketch is here reproduced; the larger one adds important details, for on the bench at the girl's side is a wash-tub, and above it a shelf, with a cat asleep. The girl was formerly said to be the Hon. Mrs. Graham (whom Gainsborough had painted in 1777, arrayed in all possible magnificence of silks, brocade, jewelry, and feathers), and the picture was thought of as an example of that fashionable rusticity which led fine ladies to play at being milkmaids and shepherdesses. Sir Joshua had painted the Hon. Mrs. Pelham feeding chickens in a farmyard, and Gainsborough had represented Elizabeth Linley and her handsome brother Tom in rags, as though they were beggars or gipsies. But no painter would have represented the Hon. Mrs. Graham as a housemaid with a broom, unless he had been commissioned to do so by the lady or by her lord. The picture was certainly never delivered to Mr. Graham, for it was among the works in Gainsborough's studio at the time of his death. The artist later made use of the sketch in his own characteristic way — a thing that he would hardly have been bold enough to do, had not the conception been wholly his own. The cottage-girl with the broom appears again as a detail in a large landscape of 1786, where she is one of a number of figures animating the scene. Behind her sits the cottager's wife, nursing a baby, and in front is her sister feeding pigs.[2] Clearly this is no maid in a well-to-do household.

If, as seems probable, the painter's genius had been awakened by the glimpse of a girl at her cottage-door, a place to which he now turned instinctively for inspiration, how significant is this

[1] See *Studies of Figures selected from the Sketch Books of the late Thomas Gainsborough in exact imitation of the original drawings*, by Richard Lane, London, 1825, No. 1. The book contains six sketches of peasants, most of which were never used again.

[2] The oil painting, which is in the possession of Lord Tollemache, was shown at the Burlington Exhibition in 1934. It measures $38\frac{3}{4}'' \times 48\frac{3}{4}''$.

GAINSBOROUGH.   CHARITY RELIEVING DISTRESS
From the painting in the possession of William Ziegler, Esq.

sketch! Here was a type of beauty, 'simplex munditiis,' plain in its neatness, of a kind very different from that which habitually appeared in the artist's studio, filled with pretentious people in fine clothes.

'The Cottage-Door' has a sort of companion-piece, which, commonly called 'The Beggars,' would be more appropriately entitled, 'The Castle-Door.'[1] It was probably painted about 1784. In it there is an almost perfect balance between the village scene (with cathedral tower in the background) and the human beings (eleven in all) who lend interest to it. A peasant woman with five small children receives a plate of food, poured into her eldest boy's hat, from the servant at the door of the house. Two fine young ladies watch the scene, as does a village-boy seated on the steps that lead up to the terrace. The original sketch for this scene, lacking many of the details (the young ladies at the door and the rider on the ass), was shown at the Gainsborough Exhibition in 1936; but the completed picture, which is now in New York,[2] has not, I think, been reproduced before. Certain details give it, oddly enough, a Spanish look; but the cathedral tower in the background is re-assuringly English.

These pictures had been preceded by one of the most important of the series, a 'Shepherd-Boy in a Storm,' exhibited in 1781, and engraved immediately afterwards (October, 1781). Intensely sentimental, it had, perhaps for that very reason, a great success. Of this picture Hazlitt, who did not care deeply for Gainsborough, wrote (though his eye could hardly have been on the picture as he did so):[3]

Nor can too much praise be given to his Shepherd Boy in a Storm, in which the unconscious simplicity of the boy's expression, looking up with his hands folded and with timid wonder — the noisy chattering of a magpie perched above — and the rustling of the coming storm in the branches of the trees — produce a most delightful and romantic impression on the mind.

[1] When the picture was exhibited at Schomberg House in 1784, it was called 'Charity relieving Distress.'
[2] In the possession of Mr. William Ziegler, who has courteously permitted me to use it here.
[3] *Painting and the Fine Arts*, 1838, pp. 37–38.

GAINSBOROUGH.   SHEPHERD-BOY IN A STORM

From the engraving by Richard Earlom, 1781

Delighted with his success, Gainsborough continued to paint in this manner until the end. Like Sir Joshua, he still turned out portraits as well, but his passion was divided between landscape, to which he had never proved false, and this newly-adopted genre-painting. This was his romantic escape into a world where the imagination might have play, and where his memories of the lanes and hedges of Suffolk, in which he had left his heart, might be re-created in ideal form. If this kind of painting happened to co-incide with a fashionable taste for a simpler existence, so much the better; for he, like most true artists, had never pretended to be indifferent to the tide of fashion and to the sale of his pictures.

One of the best of these genre-pictures in America is Mrs. Harkness's 'Children gathering Wood' (recently shown at the Metropolitan Museum), the small oil sketch for which is in the National Gallery. The seated boy, with sticks in his lap, is a favourite model, who appears in several pictures. The smoking chimney of the cottage to which the children belong is in the middle distance. A few sheep constitute their father's humble flock. Such are the short and simple annals of the poor which Gainsborough, no doubt, found within easy walking distance of Schomberg House, but the sentiment for which had entered his heart long before in the days of his youth. Of cottages Gains-borough always spoke with affection. Sir Uvedale Price, in refer-ring to a period long before this, while the artist was still living at Bath, remarks:

Though of a lively and playful imagination, yet was he at times severe and sarcastic, but when we have come near to cottages and village scenes with groups of children, and objects of rural life that struck his fancy, I have observed his countenance to take an expression of gentle-ness and complacency.[1]

And in a letter to Sir William Chambers, written during the period of his genre-paintings, Gainsborough himself wrote:

If I can pick pockets in the portrait way two or three years longer, I intend to sneak into a cot, and turn a serious fellow.[2]

This sentiment is of course playful. Gainsborough would hardly have been comfortable in a cottage after his long sojourn in Bath

---

[1] W. T. Whitley, *Thomas Gainsborough*, p. 41.   [2] Whitley, p. 204.

GAINSBOROUGH.   JACK HILL IN HIS COTTAGE

From the engraving by C. Turner, 1809

and the west end of London; but, like other men, he enjoyed the dream of living according to Nature, and looked with eyes of affection upon the rural life of England.

The interior of a cottage is painted in a picture (known to me only through engravings of it) sometimes called 'Jack Hill in his Cottage.' In front of a blazing fire are two peasant children and a cat: the boy warming his hands, and the girl seated, eating her supper of bread and milk from a bowl. Extreme poverty is here insisted upon, for the barefoot children are in rags, and in the window are the jug and the broken loaf from which have come the supper of the little girl. In the casement is a robin, which may very well have come into the picture from Thomson's 'Winter,' where the poet describes the redbreast, who

> pays to trusted man
> His annual visit. Half afraid, he first
> Against the window beats; then, brisk, alights
> On the warm hearth.

These pictures, like Sir Joshua's 'fancy' pieces, were, as a rule, not commissioned, but painted to please the artist himself, and are therefore of the greater significance to us. Jack Hill, the boy who posed for the central figure, is the subject of a companion-piece, in which he stands with his cat in front of a broken fence,[1] barefoot, and clothed, as here, only in a miserable shift. This cat, which was admired in the eighteenth century, reminds us that Gainsborough was the best — one may perhaps safely say the only — eighteenth century English painter of this admirable domestic creature.[2]

Gainsborough was probably not unaware that a charge of sentimentality may be brought against these pictures. He therefore sometimes adopted a brusquer tone, as though insisting that he is no mere dreamer. In the canvas called 'Girl and Pigs,' the poverty, which he had never understated, is made conspicuous.[3]

---

[1] The picture, now in the Metropolitan Museum, has darkened, and is seldom shown.

[2] Excellent studies of a cat were shown in the Cincinnati Art Museum at the Gainsborough Exhibition in 1931.

[3] The picture is, I believe, at Castle Howard; the scene is used as a detail in the landscape owned by Lord Tollemache.

GAINSBOROUGH. GIRL AND PIGS

From an engraving by Richard Earlom, 1783

GAINSBOROUGH.   OLD HORSE
From the painting in the Tate Gallery

This picture, which caused a sensation when it was exhibited at the Academy in 1782, as it represents a barefoot girl watching a group of pigs eating from a bowl, was purchased by no less a person that Sir Joshua Reynolds himself. The great President, in whose compliments there is often a touch of innuendo, remarked that it was 'by far the best picture that he [Gainsborough] ever painted or perhaps ever will.' Sir Joshua was fully, even sympathetically, aware of what his great rival was doing, and, as we shall see, even ventured to compete with him in this style. In his fourteenth Discourse, delivered in 1788, after the death of Gainsborough and devoted entirely to an analysis and eulogy of his work, Reynolds mentions in particular 'the interesting simplicity and elegance of his little ordinary beggar-children.'

If, in his walks, he found a character that he liked, and whose attendance was to be obtained, he ordered him to his house: and from the fields he brought into his painting-room stumps of trees, weeds, and animals of various kinds; and designed them, not from memory, but immediately from the objects.

In this instance he actually had three pigs in his studio while painting the picture.

In his fancy-pictures, when he had fixed on his object of imitation, whether it was the mean and vulgar form of a wood-cutter, or a child of an interesting character, as he did not attempt to raise the one, so neither did he lose any of the natural grace and elegance of the other; such a grace and such an elegance, as are more frequently found in cottages than in courts.

In an ambitious hour, Sir Joshua, at the invitation of Thomas Macklin, who was creating a gallery of pictures illustrative of the English poets, undertook to emulate his great rival and depict a group of peasants at the cottage-door. The picture, painted after Gainsborough's death, variously called 'The Cottagers,' 'The Gleaner,' and 'The Macklin Family,' represents a woman spinning at the cottage-door, a daughter feeding chickens, and another — the 'gleaner'— in the centre of the scene, with a sheaf upon her head. But Reynolds, though he had painted handsome pictures of shepherds, babes in the wood, and even beggars, had no instinctive love of peasants to inspire him. His models were Mrs. Macklin, her daughter, and a Miss Potts (afterwards Mrs. Landseer, the mother of the famous animal-painter). According to Macklin's catalogue of the pictures exhibited in his gallery, the scene illustrates a passage in James Thomson's 'Autumn,'[1] which describes life according to Nature in the most extravagant and romantic terms:

> Here too dwells simple truth, plain innocence,
> Unsullied beauty, sound unbroken youth,
> Patient of labour — with a little pleased,
> Health ever-blooming, unambitious toil.

Reynolds considered that Gainsborough's 'Girl and Pigs' had but one defect — the girl was not sufficiently beautiful. He preferred a smooth and regular beauty, certain of its sentimental appeal, and, in order to achieve it, painted not peasant women but ladies playing at rusticity. But Gainsborough was sick of fine ladies, and devoted himself more and more to an austerer kind of subject. Such a canvas is his portrait of an old white horse, now almost beyond service, a picture in his studio at the time of his death.[2] It is a picture without a trace of beauty, without anything to commend it to the sentimental spectator. Yet it might serve as an illustration for Burns's 'Auld Farmer's Salutation to his Auld Mare, Maggie,' a poem from the Kilmarnock volume (1786), which must be almost exactly contemporaneous with the picture. Like Burns, Gainsborough was fond of all the domestic animals, and introduced them with great frequency even into his grandest pictures. In the style of painting here under consideration, they are almost never omitted. One of his genre-pictures represents two cottage-children with a donkey ('Children and Ass,' exhibited in 1785). In this affection for the dumb creation, he is at one with his great contemporary, William Cowper.

In the picture that followed 'Girl and Pigs,' Gainsborough, breaking sharply the tradition of loveliness, adopted a brutal realism of manner. It is a large canvas, called 'Shepherd-Boys

---

[1] Lines 1259–1276.

[2] The picture is now in the Tate Gallery, though it is not always exhibited. It is said to represent Gainsborough's own nag. It is one of the few pictures which Mrs. Gainsborough never sold.

GAINSBOROUGH. SHEPHERD-BOYS WITH FIGHTING DOGS

From an engraving by Birche, 1791

with Fighting Dogs' (exhibited 1783), now at Ken Wood. Though painted in the artist's most luscious style, the subject is as repellent as if it had been conceived in the Low Countries a century before; and no sooner was it exhibited than the painter was accused of having taken his fighting dogs from Snyders; but Gainsborough, who had used a similar subject years before, had no need to look across the Channel for subjects, and when he was no longer able to defend himself, the charge was answered for him by Sir Joshua Reynolds in his discourse before the Academy:

This excellence [his realism] was his own, the result of his particular observation and taste; for this he was certainly not indebted to the Flemish school, nor indeed to any school; for his grace was not academical or antique, but selected by himself from the great school of nature.

Nevertheless the picture does exemplify Gainsborough's growing sympathy with the Dutch School, in which the artist will not be deterred from representing any scene or event in our common life, however mean. The boy whose dog is getting the worst of it has raised his stick to beat the animals apart, but is stopped by the other, who sees that his own beast will come off victorious. But it is a disagreeable picture, and, though still in brilliant condition, has few admirers to-day. I think that it must be the artist's impulsive retort to those who had come to think of him as a mere reflector of elegance and grace; and some colour is given to this assumption by Gainsborough's playful assertion that his next picture should show the boys fighting and the dogs looking on.

Gainsborough's last picture, which has the sad distinction of closing the series, is known as 'The Woodman,' and is referred to, indirectly, by Sir Joshua in the passage quoted above. It was a large canvas, seven and a half feet high, and over five feet wide. The model was a blacksmith, worn out by a life of toil, who had sunk to be dependent on casual charity. On its completion and exhibition, it was rumoured that it would be added by the King to the royal collection; but George III's patronage of art, like his sanity, was drawing to a close, and the intention, if he had ever had it, was not carried out. The picture, which remained unsold at the painter's death in 1788, was engraved posthumously in 1791. The painting is referred to in Gainsborough's last letter to

GAINSBOROUGH. THE WOODMAN

From an engraving by Simon, 1791

Reynolds, written from his death-bed, in which he begs of the President 'a last favor.' This, wrote the dying man, is 'to come once more under my roof, and look at my things. My "Woodman" you never saw.' Did Reynolds, when he saw the picture, think that the old peasant should have been made more beautiful? Gainsborough, perhaps, meant his friend and rival to see in it the conclusion towards which these humbler subjects had been tending. Poverty has here no amelioration, no soft and winning touch of ideality. The old man puts one in mind of the poetry of George Crabbe, 'Nature's sternest painter, yet the best.' Typical is the very cur that cowers at the peasant's side — an eloquent contrast to the fine collie in the earlier 'Shepherd-Boy,' to which this picture is a strange pendant.

Mrs. Gainsborough sold 'The Woodman' to Lord Gainsborough of Exton Park, Cobham, where the picture was burned with the rest of the peer's collection in 1810. It is known to us through the contemporary engraving (here reproduced) and from what I take to be the original sketch ($23\frac{1}{2}'' \times 15\frac{1}{2}''$) formerly in the possession of Sir Charles Holmes. It is a misfortune that the completed picture should have been destroyed, since it is in truth a prelude to the work of that poet who was to make Michael, Simon Lee, and the Old Cumberland Beggar familiar names in the history of poetry.

Over forty years had passed since William Collins had written of the consummate grace of simplicity,

> Though taste, though genius bless
> To some divine excess,
> Faints the cold work till Thou inspire the whole!

In the interval many attempts had been made to achieve this simplicity in painting, but none had come nearer to success than Gainsborough in these pictures of peasants, beggars, and cottage-children. He died in 1788, feeling that he had only begun to realise his powers in this regard. It was exactly ten years later that the ideal of utter simplicity was embodied in the *Lyrical Ballads*, two stanzas of which express the very sentiments of Gainsborough in the pictures here passed in review:

> I met a little cottage Girl:
>   She was eight years old, she said;
> Her hair was thick with many a curl
>   That clustered round her head.
>
> She had a rustic, woodland air,
>   And she was wildly clad:
> Her eyes were fair and very fair;
>   — Her beauty made me glad.

NOTE ON GAINSBOROUGH'S GENRE–PAINTINGS

There is no adequate critical treatment and no complete list of these pictures. There is the initial difficulty of distinguishing them from the landscape-paintings, out of which they naturally developed, such as 'Returning from Market' (in Miss Hanna's Collection, Cincinnati) or Lord Swaythling's more familiar 'Harvest Waggon' (1775?). In addition to the paintings mentioned in the text, certain other examples are well-known, such as 'Girl with Dog and Pitcher' (1785, in Lady Beit's Collection), 'Girl gathering Mushrooms' (shown at the Exhibition of British Country Life, 1937), 'Peasant Children' (Walters Gallery); and the two pictures contributed to Macklin's Gallery, 'Lavinia,' illustrating the familiar incident in Thomson's 'Summer,' and 'Young Hobbinol.' The last two I have never seen, nor those referred to by Whitley as 'Girl with Sticks' (1782) and 'Beggar Boys' (1785). The number will be greatly increased by including the peasant-subjects in the drawings. Such are the 'Faggot-Gatherers' (two versions) and another 'Woodman' (seated on a pile of faggots), and those reproduced by Lane in *Studies of Figures from the Sketch Books of Thomas Gainsborough*, two volumes, London, 1825.

V

BLAKE: 'THE GATES OF PARADISE'

PERHAPS because of his isolated position in the history of eighteenth century poetry, William Blake is often thought of as a spiritual recluse in a world of visions, uninfluenced by the events of his age. But the most clearly defined period in his poetic career, beginning with the *Songs of Innocence* in 1789, and closing with the *Songs of Experience* in 1794, corresponds, significantly enough, with the duration of the French Revolution, and is not unrelated to it.[1] In this period Blake published also certain of the 'prophetic' books, which, for the average reader, are somewhat less impalpable than the later works. Two of these, *The Marriage of Heaven and Hell* (1790), and *America* (1793) — both of course etched and illuminated in Blake's peculiar fashion — I mention since they are of use in interpreting the series of engravings known as the *Gates of Paradise* (1793).

It is ironical that a book should appear at the beginning of this period with the title, *Songs of Innocence*, and in the highest degree appropriate that at its conclusion should stand the *Songs of Experience*. This second book has a frontispiece symbolic of its central meaning, 'Youth advancing to Experience.' It is expressive of the task set the human spirit of preserving its unity by reconciling the diverse tendencies of life. Innocence and experience, for example, are opposites which must somehow be harmonised if the soul is to

---

[1] The juvenile *Poetical Sketches* (1783) are hardly to be associated with this later and more clearly defined period.

In 1791, he wrote and found a publisher for a poem over three hundred lines long entitled *The French Revolution*; it is called 'Book the First,' and carries an announcement that the remaining books are finished, and will be published in their order — an intention that was never realised. Blake was also at work upon a *Song of Liberty*, dedicated to the new spirit of freedom stirring in the world, certain passages in which unite the poetic and prophetic manners in perfect harmony:

'The son of fire in his eastern cloud, while the morning plumes her golden breast,
Spurning the clouds written with curses, stamps the stony law to dust, loosing the eternal
    horses from the dens of night, crying:

Empire is no more! and now the lion and wolf shall cease.'

BLAKE.   INNOCENCE ADVANCING TO EXPERIENCE

Frontispiece to *Songs of Experience*

receive the rewards of both these contrary states. One cannot and should not evade experience, but one must contrive that it should not defeat and destroy innocence, since the two may be reconciled in a higher spiritual unity. This, I take it, is the significance of the title of Blake's prophetic rhapsody, *The Marriage of Heaven and Hell*. From Heaven is derived the pure white truth which the soul knows by instinct; from Hell that dark and selfish but indispensable worldly wisdom which bears upon it the stamp of a lower origin. We have eaten of the fruit of the Tree of the Knowledge of Good and Evil, and it is our task, while in the flesh, to see that spiritual perception is not eclipsed by that knowledge; but that we, like Dante, may learn to envisage both in a philosophy or religion, and an active belief in the providence of God. The lion and the lamb must lie down together, and a child must lead them.[1]

In *Songs of Experience*, a poem entitled 'The Clod and the Pebble' begins:

> Love seeketh not itself to please,
>> Nor for itself hath any care,
> But for another gives its ease,
>> And builds a Heaven in Hell's despair.

Here is a Christian truth so obvious that it might be used as a copy-book maxim. It is the utterance of Innocence, a reflection of divine Truth, but it is at odds with Experience, whose voice is now heard to utter a truth that has nothing of innocence or simplicity about it:

> So sung a little clod of clay,
>> Trodden with the cattle's feet,
> But a pebble of the brook
>> Warbled out these metres meet:

> 'Love seeketh only self to please,
>> To bind another to its delight,
> Joys in another's loss of ease,
>> And builds a Hell in Heaven's despite.'

---

[1] One section of the *Marriage of Heaven and Hell*, a series of maxims or *sententiae*, is entitled, 'Proverbs of Hell':

> The road of excess leads to the palace of wisdom.
> If the fool would persist in his folly, he would become wise.
> Where man is not, Nature is barren.

Here innocence and experience merge into wisdom.

Such is romantic love, the passion that binds and blinds, and leads us to capture and enslave. Both views, though seemingly contradictory, are utterly and everlastingly true, and we must make what we can of these opposites. Wherever we turn in *Songs of Experience*, there are conflicting views presented for such reconciliation as we may be able to discover between the 'two contrary states of the human soul.' Thus in the famous poem on the 'tyger,' a counterpart of the poem on the lamb, the question is asked:

> When the stars threw down their spears,
> And watered heaven with their tears,
> Did He smile his work to see?
> Did He who made the lamb make thee?

Professor Damon has pointed out that the opening poem in *Songs of Innocence*, usually called 'The Piper,' 'tells of a song repeated thrice: first causing laughter, then tears, and finally tears of joy. Pure laughter is Innocence; tears are Experience; the third stage is Wisdom. In the two parts of his book Blake furnishes the reader with two versions of most of the songs, one of laughter, one of tears, and leaves the synthesis — the third stage, Wisdom — to the reader.' [1] Tiger and lamb, rose and worm, angel and demon, heaven and hell, childhood and age, joy and tears — Blake would have us learn from one as from the other.

With *Songs of Innocence and of Experience* and the contrasted views which they embody must be associated the series of small engravings which have the odd title, *For Children: The Gates of Paradise*, a title made yet stranger by the fact, now, I think, generally accepted, that Blake originally intended to issue a sequel, to be called *The Gates of Hell*. As it is, the pictures are often hellish enough, but they represent scenes which must be passed before the gates of Paradise are attained. The dedication of the volume to little children makes it stranger still. Mr. Wicksteed goes so far as to assert that, in the *Gates of Paradise*, 'we see the whole of human life before and after birth, and even after death, represented as sordid and tragic, with one great break through into Eternity (Plate 13).' [2]

---

[1] Damon reviewing Wicksteed's edition of *Songs of Innocence and of Experience*, *Saturday Review of Literature*, March 30, 1929.

[2] Wicksteed, *Blake's Innocence and Experience*, p. 47, note 2.

This, surely, is too extreme, for the pictures, though often terrible, are always arresting, and often romantic and ennobling, as tragic themes invariably are.

The little book, which contains in all eighteen plates,[1] touches the profoundest problems of life; but the truths set forth are not the innate ideas of Innocence. The pictures, about which there is nothing childlike, are inspired by thoughts as paradoxical as those in *Songs of Experience*. The use of small engraved pictures for such a purpose recalls the emblems of an earlier century, and reminds us that *The Gates of Paradise* is, in brief, an emblem-book.

I use the terms 'emblem' and 'emblem-book' in the technical sense.[2] An emblem-book is a series of small pictures (usually engravings) of symbolic character, together with gnomic sentences (often in verse), proverbs, maxims, or the like,[3] which profess to interpret the scene represented, but often only emphasise its difficulty. In emblem-books the pictures are always of the first importance; it is for them that the proverbs and maxims exist. It is the startling character of the picture which first catches the attention and piques the curiosity of the child. In earlier emblem-books the grotesque mingles with the simple, and the figurative language of the Bible, as in the Psalms and Canticles, is set forth literally and crudely in scenes drawn from the common life of the people. Romance issues out of realism.

Although vivid, emblems are never obvious, but deal with profound matters. In England and in New England they were prevailingly religious, and exposed the perils of man among the deceits and vanities of a transitory world. Even in amatory emblems, which disclose the pitfalls along the lover's pathway, there is a serious deposit of truth, based on the experience of the race, which no man can ignore with impunity.

That Blake, trained as an engraver, had been familiar with

---

[1] The title-page is omitted from the reproductions here given.

[2] Gilchrist in his *Life of Blake* (1880), vol. I, p. 99, refers to the engravings as emblems; so does Sampson in his edition of Blake's *Poems*, p. 367.

[3] *Emblemata selectiora. Typis elegantissimis expressa, nec non sententiis, carminibus, historiis, ac proverbiis, ex scriptoribus cum sacris tum profanis, antiquis et recentioribus illustrata.*

This, the title of an emblem-book published at Amsterdam in 1704, well describes the type.

emblem-books in his childhood need not, I think, be doubted.[1] It is true that a man with so active an imagination as his had no need to turn to them for inspiration; but he must have been aware that in *The Gates of Paradise* he was employing a well-known literary and artistic type. As an emblem-book it naturally depicted scenes beyond the comprehension of a child; but it was sufficient that the pictures should startle and waylay, stimulate the imagination of the young, and tax the ingenuity of the mature. Emblems are never graded down to the level of the childish mind, but made so vivid that children may learn to love them first and understand them later.

Blake's little book had no success — none of his publications was really popular in his own lifetime — but many years later, probably between 1805 and 1810, he re-issued it with certain minor changes in the plates and with additional comments, called 'The Keys of the Gates,' which, being worded in Blake's cryptic style, are not always illuminating.[2] To this issue he now gave the title, *For the Sexes: the Gates of Paradise*. This change I do not pretend to account for, since the book hardly seems more appropriate to young lovers than to young children. But to whomever it is addressed, the subject remains of the last importance, for it illustrates the pilgrimage of the Soul through a hostile world.

The vast mysteries which Man, with his perceptions darkened by his material existence —'the mundane shell,' as Blake was later to call it — encounters in his worldly life, are here depicted with a novelty and a power which rival the artist's most impressive productions. The pictures are, to be sure, little more than vignettes, tiny line-engravings in black and white, without the added charm of Blake's colouring, and without any of the visionary personages who were to be so prominent in the prophetic books.

[1] There are at least two of Blake's emblems in *The Gates of Paradise* which repeat motives from earlier emblem-books: the tenth, depicting the soul of man drowning in the sea of Time; and the eleventh, which shows Old Age (or, possibly, Time) clipping the wings of Love. With the former compare Quarles, Book III, emblem 9; and with the latter *Amorum Emblemata*, Antwerp, 1612, p. 237.

[2] The differences between the two issues are fully dealt with by Keynes in his *Bibliography of William Blake*, p. 173. A fac-simile of *For the Sexes* was published by Mr. W. A. White, for private distribution, many years ago. From this the reproductions here used have been taken.

There are no angels or demons, no 'zoas' or emanations, no Albion or Urizen, no shadowy Urthona or red Orc. These were to come later, and to have a part in a system of thought that had become mystical and philosophical rather than poetic. But in 1794, when the emblem-book was first published, Blake, though at the height of his powers as a draughtsman, and though living already an intensely imaginative life, was not yet in the prophetic or visionary state; so that it is not impossible, even for those of us who fail to comprehend his later work, to attain an appreciation of the hidden meaning in these emblems. Even if something of their author's intention eludes us, as is not unlikely, we shall have made acquaintance with a group of symbols which, like all true works of art, may contain a subtler meaning than any that their author deliberately put into them. It is a higher tribute to Blake to find a significance in his work which shall serve our own needs than to understand and adopt his peculiar system of thought. Even if one's interpretation be inadequate, or at times demonstrably false, no real harm is done by receiving Blake's pictures into the heart as well as into the mind.

The frontispiece and the first of the emblems deal with the mystery of birth; the soul of man is typified in the former as a cocoon, with the head of a sleeping infant, and in the other as a mandrake plucked out of the earth by a woman. The comparison of a human being to a worm is neither unusual nor inappropriate, and the butterfly, or *imago* in its second state, as a symbol of the resurrection of the body, is common in mediaeval allegory; but the representation of the soul as asleep in its chrysalis, like a baby in the womb, is, so far as I am aware, original with Blake. This frontispiece illustrates the mingled grotesqueness and seriousness of the typical emblem-book, for despite its comic appearance, the little picture suggests the invisible growth of the soul towards a higher plane of existence, where it will have freer activity and larger powers.

The emblem which represents a woman, who already carries a baby in her bosom, as pulling another out of the earth by its hair, is still more grotesque, a note which the legend, 'I found him beneath a tree,' does nothing to dispel. The tree of life, at whose roots the child is found, is a weeping willow; for the infant comes to birth in the sorrowful world of the four elements, out of which it has grown, as a plant develops out of the ground, where the secret of its birth lies hid.

To the symbolic presentment of the four elements, therefore, the poet now proceeds, and surprisingly repellent it is.

Water, the first in order, is typified by an old and naked man sitting on a rock, under the bare boughs of a tree, in a deluge of rain. The man, who watches with despair the rising waters at his feet, which will presently engulf him, is sometimes said to stand for the last survivor of Noah's Flood, and no injury, I think, is done by such an interpretation, since the misery of the creature's condition and his approaching extinction are only emphasised thereby; but it is equally appropriate to read the picture allegorically, and to perceive in the rising billows that sea of human woe which we, on the earthly plane, must watch as an ever-mounting tide, until at last we are swallowed up. The words under the picture, added in the second impression, 'Thou waterest him with tears,' reinforce the notion that the waters are indicative of human sorrows.

Earth is a woebegone man desperately fighting his way out of a crevice in the rocks.[1] To modern eyes it might seem to illustrate that instinctive dread of enclosure within narrow walls with which the new psychology has familiarised us; but Blake's meaning is far deeper than this. It is suggested by the words added to the plate in the later impression, 'He struggles into Life.' To the soul on its spiritual pilgrimage the body is a prison, like the Platonic cave in which man sits chained, with his back to the light. Here he is engaged in a heart-breaking effort to force his way upward to another world.

Air is a youth seated upon a cloud, in a state of distraction, or perhaps of incipient madness. He clasps his knitted brows in a frenzy of hopeless meditation, for he is reposing (as the words 'for the sexes' make clear) upon 'cloudy doubts and reasoning cares.' The insoluble problem of human existence, the questions of whence and whither, which man is ever trying to answer by means of his

---

[1] The scene is repeated in the *First Book of Urizen*, in the plate, 'Urizen enclosed among Rocks.'

What is Man!

I found him beneath
a Tree

Water

Earth

Air

Fire

At length for hatch-
ing ripe he breaks
the shell

Alas!

My Son, my Son!

BLAKE.   VIGNETTES

From *The Gates of Paradise*, 1793

I want! I want!

Help! Help!

Aged Ignorance

Does thy God O Priest
take such vengeance
as this?

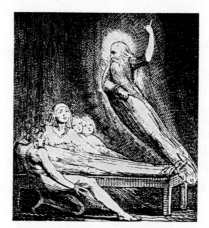

Fear & Hope are — Vision

The Traveller hasteth
in the Evening

Death's Door

I have said to the Worm:
Thou art my Mother &
my Sister

BLAKE.   VIGNETTES

From *The Gates of Paradise*, 1793

reason, which the mind is incapable of answering, and which, nevertheless, it cannot put aside — this is the cause of a soul-destroying despair. It is as though a man were to try to feed and sustain himself upon air.

Fire, an athletic spirit, standing in the midst of flames, with shield and brandished spear, is similar to the figure which Blake later used in his illustrations of the Book of Job, to represent Satan himself. In the later impression of the plates, his aimless passion is represented by his sightless eyes. This Loki-like creature stands, as do his three predecessors, for more than the mere element which is his outward manifestation; for he represents the fiery destructiveness of wrath and its dissensions, which 'end in endless strife.'

Although the four elements have been a favourite subject with artists time out of mind, it is uncommon to find them shown as cruel and menacing. Yet here they are surely both horrible and dangerous, always hostile to man, and likely to destroy him unless he finds some way of controlling their power.[1] Man, who should be their master rather than their slave, may find that their hostility will cease upon a higher plane, when their apparent enmity will be merged into the perfect harmony of Man's new life. Such, at least, is Blake's conception. If it be conceded that the only true existence is ideal or spiritual, and that the manifestations of the material world, received through the five senses, are misleading, and certainly inadequate guides to Truth, the opening of the gates of Paradise may be successfully attempted.

Man early becomes conscious of the fact that he is not merely mundane, and that the material world, hostile though it be, cannot, even in this stage of his existence, imprison the aspiring soul, which in the innocence of early childhood, breaks through its shell, and emerges into independent life. The cherub breaking from the egg in the sixth emblem is the same figure that sits on the shoulders

---

[1] Professor Percival explains the cause for this hostility: '[Blake] identifies the Zoas, in their failure to co-operate in the well-being of man, with the four elements to which man is subject. With the separation of the elements from Albion, he ceases to be their master and becomes their prey. The appearance of the four elements with the Fall is traditional. . . . A prey to the elements which beset him — his own powers in a state of contention — Albion is, like Adam, blind to the kingdom of God.' — *William Blake's Circle of Destiny*, p. 19.

of Youth in the frontispiece to *Songs of Experience*, and here, as there, represents Innocence advancing to Experience. The child is as yet perfectly joyous, and, in full confidence, looks upward to the light. So, in the well-known poem in the *Songs of Experience*, Blake addresses the sunflower which aspires to the heavens:

> Ah, Sunflower, weary of Time,
>   Who countest the steps of the Sun,
> Seeking after that sweet golden clime,
>   Where the traveller's journey is done;
>
> Where the Youth pined away with desire,
>   And the pale Virgin shrouded in snow,
> Arise from their graves and aspire
>   Where my Sunflower wishes to go.

Such is the natural instinct of the soul to come into its full inheritance; but youth falls an easy prey to the foolish and deceitful aims which prevail in the world, and which are depicted in the four succeeding plates.

The first of the four, number seven in the series, shows a boy trying to catch in his hat, not a butterfly, but a fairy on the wing.[1] That he desires her only for his selfish pleasure may be inferred from the fact that the body of another lies dead on the ground at his feet. The vanity, selfishness, and cruelty of young love are here depicted. Blake expressed the thought in a quatrain found in the Rossetti Manuscript:[2]

> He who bends to himself a joy
> Does the winged life destroy;
> But he who kisses the joy as it flies
> Lives in Eternity's sunrise.

No less cruel is the attitude of youth towards its parents, when, forgetful of the past, it turns upon its father the sting of ingratitude. The words, 'My son, my son!', printed below the next emblem, indicate that the picture was suggested by the story of David and Absalom. The aged father, with a useless sword in hand, is

---

[1] In the second stanza of *Europe, a Prophecy*, (1794), the poet tells how he saw a fairy, sitting on a streaked tulip, and how he caught him in his hat, 'as boys knock down a butterfly.'

[2] Keynes, *Writings of William Blake*, vol. I, p. 241.

threatened with death by his own child, who aims a dart at his open breast. The counterpart of this scene is expressed in the eleventh emblem, 'Aged Ignorance.'

Absalom's ingratitude was the offspring of his vaulting ambitions, and therefore the next emblem (number nine) depicts the aspiration of youth to scale, as it were, the very heavens, even if it have no other means of ascent than the frail ladder of human reason. As the moonstruck youth begins his mad climb, he is watched by two lovers, who, we may infer, have discovered another pathway to Paradise. This emblem of the passionate desire of man to comprehend the world in which he lives —'I want, I want!'— is the most widely known of all the emblems, and needs no special interpretation.

But the attempt to mount the heavens must fail, and in the tenth emblem the youth is seen to have fallen, and to be struggling for life in the water. In the Sea of Doubt and Fear, he stretches an arm to the starless sky, and cries to be delivered, like David, *de profundis* — a scene which was later to engage the pencil of Blake, 'He sent down from on high to fetch me, and took me out of many waters.'

It is not only youth which Blake satirises. The stupidity and anguish of old age also claim his attention, and in the eleventh emblem we see Aged Ignorance clipping the wings of young Love. Here the folly of age is shown in the dull and spectacled old fool, who seated under a dying tree, by the light of the sinking sun, destroys the happiness of youth. Together with its natural companion-piece, the eighth emblem, it illustrates the contrasted aims of youth and age.

But the greatest agony of man is to witness the suffering which his own folly or sin has brought upon his children. The story of Ugolino and his four sons who died of starvation in the Tower of Famine at Pisa, Blake may have derived directly from Dante (*Inferno*, XXXIII), or from Sir Joshua's picture of the same scene [1] (of which his disapproval, if he knew it, must have been violent); but this matters not. He used this design again in making his own illustrations of the *Inferno* (plate 68). The words below the emblem,

[1] See above, p. 61.

'Does thy God, O Priest, take such vengeance as this?' refer to the fact that Count Ugolino was betrayed and imprisoned by the Ghibelline leader, Ruggieri, Archbishop of Pisa. Vengeance belongs to God, and not to man. It is not impossible that Blake had read Chaucer's version of the story in the *Monk's Tale*, where the children, whose number is reduced to three, are made even more helpless and touchingly affectionate than in the *Inferno*.

In the thirteenth plate, the routine of the Pilgrim's life is suddenly shattered by vision, as is the suffering of Job, when God answers him out of the whirlwind. The Almighty appears as the man lies sick upon his bed, perhaps at the point of death. The scene is not unlike that of the appearance of God in the ninth plate of Blake's illustrations of the Book of Job, where He appears standing upon a cloud before His prostrate servant. Professor Percival, commenting on this thirteenth emblem, says: 'Lying upon his couch, he has a vision of the poetic or prophetic spirit later personified as Los. This vision permits him to "close the labours of his day" in peace. The analogue in the Job series is plate 12, where the spirit of prophecy appears, following the vision of fear — which is again the crisis, the turning point — in the preceding plate. In both series fear and hope result in vision.' [1]

Man goeth forth to his work and to his labour until the evening, but hastens homeward at the close of day. The symbol of the later life of man (number 14), showing the Pilgrim approaching with accelerating speed the goal of his earthly existence, is the simplest and certainly not the least impressive of the vignettes.

At last the old man, with bent form and trembling step, leaning upon a crutch, enters the tomb, 'Death's door' (plate 15). A wind, blowing upon his hair and robe, seems to be sweeping him into the grave, towards which he has been of late a weary but not unwilling traveller.

But this is not the end. A final scene reveals the shrouded figure of the soul, wand in hand, seated underground, below the

---

[1] I quote these words from a private letter of Professor Percival. He adds, 'The analogue in the *Four Zoas* is in Book VII, where Los and Enitharmon behold a vision of Christ.' I owe my realisation of the significance of this thirteenth plate entirely to the explanation of Professor Percival. Further elucidations of Blake may be found in his *William Blake's Circle of Destiny*, Columbia University Press, 1938.

twisting roots of a tree, with a vast worm coiling about its feet. Below the picture are the words of Job (xvii. 14), 'I have said to the worm, thou art my mother and my sister.' As the frontispiece had shown the caterpillar of life, the last emblem shows the worm of death. And yet there is here but slight suggestion of decay. Bodies of the dead, to be sure, are dimly discerned; but the prisoner of the tomb is in an attitude of expectation, with eyes staring towards the heavens for the awaited light, 'My soul fleeth unto the Lord before the morning watch, I say, before the morning watch.' But, despite the poet's high meaning, the picture is not attractive, and it seems strange that Blake, whose religion was based on faith in the continuous life of the soul, should have been willing to conclude the series with such a scene as this. One would expect him to throw open the gates and reveal the next stage in man's existence; and his failure to do so is made the more noticeable by the fact that he had already published in *The Marriage of Heaven and Hell* a very striking picture of the resurrection of the body, and had made it the more conspicuous by repeating it in *America*, a work which must have been composed at the very time when he was engraving the plates for *The Gates of Paradise*.

America, then, contains the picture of the aged man entering the door of the tomb, and it corresponds in every detail with the engraving in *The Gates of Paradise*, but a tree is added, which spreads its branches to the light. This I associate with the roots, mentioned above, which thrust themselves down into the grave, and which belong, I take it, to the Tree of Life. There is nothing in *America* which corresponds with the picture of the soul sitting in the tomb; but in its place is the risen and rejuvenated soul at break of day, looking to heaven, whence the new light has come. This is an exact replica of the figure in *The Marriage of Heaven and Hell*, of which mention has been made, and the artist's own meaning is put beyond doubt by the accompanying text:

The morning comes, the night decays, the watchmen leave their stations;
The grave is burst, the spices shed, the linen wrapped up;
The bones of death, the cov'ring clay, the sinews shrunk & dry'd,
Reviving shake, inspiring move, breathing, awakening!
Spring like redeemed captives when their bonds & bars are burst;

BLAKE. DEATH'S DOOR

From *America*, 1793

Let the slave grinding at the mill, run out into the field:
Let him look up into the heavens & laugh in the bright air;
Let the inchained soul shut up in darkness and in sighing,
Whose face has never seen a smile in thirty weary years;
Rise and look out, his chains are loose, his dungeon doors are open.

This figurative language is of course from the New Testament, but
the being represented is not the risen Christ, but risen Man, who
has so completely identified himself with the Saviour [1] that he,
too, has passed through the grave and gate of Death to a joyful
resurrection.

A few years later Blake became well-known as an illustrator of
the poems of other men. He made designs, forty-three of which
were used, for an edition of Edward Young's *Night-Thoughts*,
originally published in 1742, and re-issued in 1797 by Edwards,
who advertised Blake's illuminations as a 'perfectly new style
of decoration, surrounding the text which they are designed to
elucidate.' [2] This publication, though not specially successful,
associated the artist's name with illustrations of a mystical character. In 1805 he made twelve drawings [3] for a somewhat similar
poem, *The Grave*, by Robert Blair, published in 1743, which a publisher named Cromek now proposed to reprint with engraved
plates. Among Blake's designs, which are marked by surpassing
vigour and spiritual insight, are such subjects as 'The Descent of
Man into the Vale of Death' (viii), 'The Soul exploring the Recesses of the Grave' (x), and 'The Re-union of the Soul and the
Body' (xii).

Blake had naturally expected to engrave the designs himself,
and Cromek had so agreed; but he was on the threshold of a new
career, and was timid and cautious. Blake's eccentricity, con-

---

[1] Blake's conception of the relation between Man and Christ is set forth in what is
perhaps his grandest plate (*Jerusalem*, number 76). The Redeemer is crucified to the
Tree of Life, and before him stands Albion (Man) in a posture of passionate adoration.
The scene is repeated in the illustration for *Paradise Lost*, which represents St. Michael
showing Adam the vision of Christ on the cross. Cf. 'Dante adoring Christ,' *Paradiso*,
plate 90.

[2] Keynes, *Bibliography of William Blake*, p. 202.

[3] There are thirteen plates in the book; but the frontispiece, a portrait of Blake,
is an engraving by Schiavonetti after a painting by T. Phillips. The other twelve are
from Blake's designs.

The morning comes, the night decays, the watchmen leave
        their stations;
The grave is burst, the spices shed, the linen wrapped up;
The bones of death, the covering clay, the sinews shrunk & dry'd.
Reviving shake, inspiring move, breathing! awakening!
Spring like redeemed captives when their bonds & bars are burst;
Let the slave grinding at the mill, run out into the field:
Let him look up into the heavens & laugh in the bright air;
Let the inchained soul shut up in darkness and in sighing,
Whose face has never seen a smile in thirty weary years;
Rise and look out, his chains are loose, his dungeon doors are open.
And let his wife and children return from the opressors scourge:
They look behind at every step & believe it is a dream.
Singing. The Sun has left his blackness, & has found a fresher morning
And the fair Moon rejoices in the clear & cloudless night;
For Empire is no more, and now the Lion & Wolf shall cease.

BLAKE.   RESURRECTION

From *America*, 1793

spicuous in the drawings, would, he realised, be accentuated in the engravings. He, therefore, to Blake's intense indignation, put the drawings into the hands of a gifted young Italian, Louis Schiavonetti, Bartolozzi's most brilliant pupil, whose touch as an engraver was softer and whose manner more ingratiating than Blake's. The publication was a commercial success, and has remained one of the best-known of Blake's illustrative series, though it has never had the fame of the majestic illustrations of the Book of Job, in which both drawing and engraving are by Blake. Cromek purchased his success at the expense of what was most typical, albeit indefinable, in Blake's art.

It is not improbable that Blake's work on the illustrations for Blair's *Grave* turned his thoughts back to his own *Gates of Paradise*, which itself belonged to what is somewhat derisively known as the 'Graveyard School,' and led him to change what had originally been a picture-book 'for children' into one of his prophetic works 'for the sexes.' His emblems of the tomb were certainly before his mind as he made the drawings for Blair's *Grave*, the final plate in which is none other than that 'Door of Death' which he had used in both *America* and *The Gates of Paradise*; but in this, its final form, he united it with the picture of the risen soul, and thus made the upper half of his design interpret the lower. Blake's rough drawing for this plate, now in the possession of Mr. Newton,[1] shows how Schiavonetti softened the outlines and mitigated the intensity of the original conception.

Blair's *Grave*, published in 1808, was dedicated to Queen Charlotte, to whom Blake addressed one of the best-known of his poems, which, since it makes obvious reference not only to the illustrations in that book, but to the earlier emblems as well, must be given here in its entirety:

> The Door of Death is made of gold,
> That mortal eyes cannot behold;
> But when the mortal eyes are clos'd,
> And cold and pale the limbs repos'd,
> The soul awakes; and wond'ring sees
> In her mild hand the golden Keys;

---

[1] It was used an illustration in *A Magnificent Farce*. It is here reproduced by Mr. Newton's kind permission.

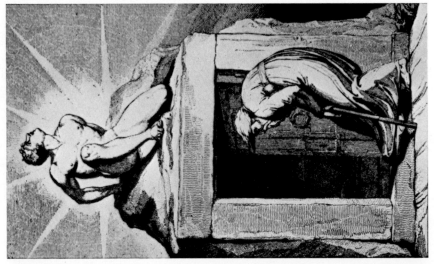

BLAKE. DEATH AND RESURRECTION

Left: Blake's pen and ink sketch for 'Death's Door'; right: Schiavonetti's engraving of it for Cromek's edition of Blair's *Grave*

The Grave is Heaven's golden Gate,
And rich and poor around it wait;
O Shepherdess of England's fold,
Behold this Gate of pearl and gold!

To dedicate to England's Queen
The visions that my soul has seen,
And, by her kind permission, bring
What I have borne on solemn wing,
From the vast regions of the Grave,
Before her throne my wings I wave;
Bowing before my Sov'reign's feet,
'The Grave produc'd these blossoms sweet
In mild repose from earthly strife;
The blossoms of Eternal Life'!

Here, then, is Blake's key to the Gates of Paradise.

VI

WILSON: SOLITUDE; THE ITALIAN TRADITION

THE very word *landscape*, itself a product of the seventeenth century, suggests a scene in a condition more or less natural, not exclusive of human beings and their works, but certainly at a remove from towered cities and the busy hum of men. A populous city street is not a landscape, but neither is the heart of a jungle nor the sandy expanse of a desert. A scene without some mark of the human presence upon it will neither please nor terrify for very long; but, on the other hand, the persons represented in it must not distract attention to their individual concerns or their immediate fate, lest the landscape represented sink to a mere background. There is about landscape-painting, in spite of its nearness to the warm earth, something of the austerity of abstract truth, since it fixes attention on man's position in the universe. It is difficult to see how reflective poetry in its amplitude or landscape-painting in its beauty can come to perfection without a love of leisurely meditation and frequent recourse to solitude. Artists and poets alike express this wish for peace,— for a 'lodge in some vast wilderness,' where the necessaries of life may be reduced to the jug and the loaf. An exponent of such solitude is the hermit, with his few books, his beads, and maple dish; and upon him the imagination of the painter has dwelt lovingly, even in ages which have belittled the holy art of meditation. The hermit, seen in relief against the vast majesty of mountain, cataract, and forest, stirs the emotion and kindles the imagination, for he is a symbol of the strangeness of our human plight,— man at bay in an alien world.

Nothing intensifies the atmosphere of solitude more than the traces of a former life, be it the colossal wreck of an empire or the pathos of an abandoned cottage; for they are alike parables of a fleeting world. Therefore landscape-painters — Claude Lorraine, Salvator Rosa, the Poussins, Pannini, Hubert Robert, and a hundred others — delight in the representation of ruins, since they shed upon the canvas a meaning not to be missed by the hastiest passer-by. In such picturesqueness no country has ever vied with Italy, where two mingled civilisations bring into eloquent contrast the ruined palace and the cell of the anchorite, the pagan temple, and the peasant's hut. It was as he sat musing at the close of evening, 'in the church of the Zoccolanti or Franciscan friars,' that Edward Gibbon conceived the idea of writing the *Decline and Fall*, 'while they were singing vespers in the temple of Jupiter on the ruins of the Capital.' The historian may have known the words of a poem, written some twenty years before, John Dyer's *Ruins of Rome*, in which a hoary monk is shown as lamenting over that solitary scene

> Where Caesars, heroes, peasants, hermits lie,
> Blended in dust together; where the slave
> Rests from his labours; where th' insulting proud
> Resigns his power; the miser drops his hoard;
> Where human folly sleeps.

But if solitude is typified by the hermit, it is typified by the bandit and the outlaw as well. Narrow defiles, threatening rocks, gloomy mountain-passes, the thunder-shattered cliff, and the blasted tree are no doubt romantic, but are the haunt of the wolf and the venomous reptile, where the benighted traveller, the lost huntsman, and the shipwrecked mariner may meet death at the turn of the path. Travellers in the seventeenth and early eighteenth centuries have less to say of the beauties of landscape than we moderns should expect of them, because their attention was often fixed on reaching their destination in safety. 'Improvements in roads and means of travel,' says Miss Manwaring,[1] 'had a great deal to do with the increasing enjoyment of scenery. In fact, a large part of what has been considered hatred or fear of mountains was well-warranted uneasiness at discomfort and danger.'

Thus the mountains of Italy supply that actual melodrama which inspires the landscapes of Salvator, while its plains preserve the gray legends of a remote past, which, half alive in the dim evening of the empire, fill the pictures of Claude Lorraine. These contrasted moods of horror and serenity, of danger and peace, find expression not only in the work of the seventeenth century

---

[1] *Italian Landscape in Eighteenth Century England*, New York, 1925, p. 7.

WILSON.   A FOUNTAIN

WILSON.   LANDSCAPE

Scenes from a sketch-book of Wilson's, made in Italy in 1752

masters of landscape, but in their disciple of the English School, Wilson, whose austere canvases recall

> Whate'er Lorraine light-touch'd with softening hue,
> Or savage Rosa dash'd, or learned Poussin drew.

Richard Wilson, often, but with doubtful propriety, called the father of English landscape-painting, was of Welsh extraction and of gentle birth. Acquainted during his formative years with the most romantic scenery in the western part of the island, he took, at the age of thirty-five, the bold step of abandoning his profession of portrait-painter in the metropolis — a profession in which he was by no means unsuccessful — and departing to Italy for a period of prolonged study. It lasted from 1749 to 1756, and resulted, as the world knows, in the devotion of his remaining years to landscape-painting. A group of sketches, made during this sojourn, has a kind of title-page, apparently in the artist's own hand, reading: *Studies & Designs by Ri. Wilson, done at Rome in y*ᵉ *Year 1752. Caffe dellé Inglesi.*[1] This invaluable sketch-book, formerly in the possession of Oldfield Bowles, reveals the impression made upon the artist by the scenery between Rome and Naples. 'He has represented,' writes Archer, 'the general character of Italy, its dreary and inhospitable plains, rendered solemnly interesting by the mouldering fragments of temples, tombs, and aqueducts, with peculiar effect. He has represented also, with equal truth, its rugged and romantic scenery.' But the impression may be more accurately defined. There is here whatever one might expect — hill-towns, stone-pines, coastal scenery, and fishing craft, the excavations at Herculaneum, and the crater of Vesuvius — but it is the singular combination of ruined magnificence with modern poverty, beauty mingling with squalor, that is perpetually before his mind's eye. He is aware of the Church in the background, but has nothing to say of it, either in praise or in blame. Of myth and legend, so dear to Claude and, later, to Turner, he has nothing to tell. There is no 'Sacrifice to Apollo,' no 'Psyche abandoned before the Palace of Eros,'[2] nothing, in short, strictly imitative in

---

[1] Published by Robert Archer, at Oxford, in 1811. I cannot explain the significance of the reference to the 'Caffe dellé Inglesi.'

[2] Known in England as 'The Enchanted Castle.'

WILSON. VILLA BORGHESE
From the painting in the possession of Captain Ford

this pleasant book. He sketches the recumbent fisherman, the wood-cutter hacking at a fallen tree, and women drawing water at a ruined fountain. This last provides an interesting hint of the close association of the peasants' daily life with the ruins by which they were surrounded.

Wilson's paintings of Italian scenes have similar details: the shapely stone-pine silhouetted against a luminous sky, a ruinous fragment of magnificent architecture, a long 'prospect,' extending far into distance, and a few human beings in pathetic contrast to the once-populous splendour of the scene. The picture of 'The Villa Borghese,' in Captain Ford's collection (shown at Amsterdam in the exhibition of 1936), has an atmosphere of loneliness about it, but nothing suggestive of danger, for it is relieved by one or two simple human touches. In the lower left-hand corner the artist himself is seated, with his sketch-book on his knees, while, to the right of the ruined arch, two tiny figures look down upon the scene. That is all; but it is enough to remove the impression of desolation. The arch itself cuts off any extensive prospect, usually found in landscapes painted in the Italian tradition.

The picture known as 'Hadrian's Villa,' in the National Gallery, illustrates the use which Wilson made of human figures in his landscapes and his attitude to the peasant-life of Italy. It might have been painted to accompany certain lines of Goldsmith, which, though published in *The Traveller* in 1764, may well have been composed during his travels on the Continent some years before:

> As in those domes, where Caesars once bore sway,
> Defac'd by time and tottering in decay,
> There in the ruin, heedless of the dead,
> The shelter-seeking peasant builds his shed,
> And, wondering man could want the larger pile,
> Exults, and owns his cottage with a smile.

Here even the cottage is falling into decay. Beneath the arch, where the goats are sheltering, a rude ladder ascends to the cottage; and the simple life of the Italian peasants is suggested by the sluggish figures in the foreground. A road winding to the right carries the eye down a long prospect to the mountain on the horizon. The

WILSON.   HADRIAN'S VILLA

From an engraving by J. Carter

human figures in this picture are as important as Wilson ever permits them to be, for he never made the artistic mistake of recom-
mending the characters to our sympathy rather than the scene
itself to our admiration. So the people recline upon rocks, lean
upon staffs, carry ewers to a fountain, hold a fishing rod over a
quiet water, or row a boat across a stream. Clearly, though the
artist regarded them as of importance in the composition of the
scene, he bestowed but little care upon them; for it would be
preposterous to suggest that he, who had excelled as a portrait-
painter, could not have made them as realistic and interesting as
he chose to have them. He, like Claude, sold the landscape (if he
could), and gave away the figures; and like Claude, again, he
permitted other painters [1] to put in the human beings if they were
essential to the story or the theme.

And yet, in these figures, there is a larger value than that which
they lend to the composition or the story. Remove them from the
scene, and its significance is impaired, for they provide the tone,
or perhaps we should say the overtone, of the picture. In them
abides the peacefulness — or the horror — of the scene. You may
paint the depths of the forest or the smiling plain, the desert or the
wilderness, but unless there is, at the centre of the scene, a tranquil
human heart, you will scarcely succeed in denoting peace. The
fanciful names which have been given to Wilson's canvases refer
to this prevalent serenity: 'Afternoon,' 'The Convent,' 'The
White Monk,' 'Landscape, with a Philosopher,' and the sentiment
is conveyed, not only by the quiet of the landscape, but by the
reposefulness of the persons in it. He seldom made the figures so
interesting as to absorb attention, lest the spectator should forget
the scene.

One of Wilson's imaginary landscapes, containing two human
beings in a prominent position in the foreground, is entitled
'Solitude,' after the engraving made from it. This, like the similar
picture known as 'The White Monk,' was a favourite subject of the
painter's, and was often repeated. Colonel Grant has in his collection no less than four versions of the scene, and there are other
repetitions. According to Woollett's engraving (1778), from which

[1] Mortimer, for example.

the illustration here used was taken, the picture was painted in
1761. It is the most 'enclosed' landscape by Wilson, lacking the
prospect so common in his pictures and in those of his Italian
predecessors. In the lower left-hand corner is a ruined statue of a
lion, of which only the tail and the hind quarters now remain in
place; the shattered head is on the ground. The two anchorets,
as in similar landscapes of Salvator Rosa, strike the keynote. Such
monastic figures were of course unknown in eighteenth century
England, but caught popular attention as something exotic and
picturesque. In the middle distance is a cross, worshipped by a
group of monks,[1] members of the order, we may suppose, to which
the two hermits in the foreground belong. No protestant prejudice
or satiric intention intrudes here or in 'The White Monk,' for Wilson was incapable of satire. The monks have no other function
than to add to the generally romantic character.

As the love of the picturesque developed in England, sham
ruins were built in order to supply the necessary Italian character
to the scene, and the 'hermitage' vied in popularity with the round
temple as a garden ornament. Miss Manwaring, in her study of
the influence of Italian landscape in England, cites the example of
Mr. Charles Hamilton, whose garden was modelled according to
the strictest Italian plan. He is 'said to have hired an old man of
venerable appearance to enliven his picture by acting as a hermit
in the hermitage at Painshill; but the hermit, wearying of visitors,
resigned his position.'[2]

'Solitude' in its engraved form, was published with a quotation from Thomson's 'Summer,' selected as giving poetical expression to the 'sacred terror,' the 'severe delight,' which the
picture was supposed to generate. If the passage was not actually
in the painter's mind when he conceived the scene, he must, at any
rate, have accepted it, when his landscape was engraved, as a
suitable commentary.

---

[1] As in pictures by Magnasco and Ricci.

[2] *Italian Landscape in Eighteenth Century England*, p. 155. The use of a hermit in an
English garden is among the amusing incidents in John O'Keeffe's *The London Hermit, or
Rambles in Dorsetshire*, acted in 1793 — a play to which Miss Manwaring has kindly
called my attention.

Still let me pierce into the midnight depth
Of yonder grove, of wildest, largest growth:
That, forming high in air a woodland quire,
Nods o'er the mount beneath. [At every step,
Solemn and slow, the shadows blacker fall,
And all is awful listening gloom around.]
    These are the haunts of Meditation, these
The scenes where antient Bards th' inspiring breath,
Extatic, felt; and, from this world retir'd,
Convers'd with angels.[1]

To converse with angels and immortal forms is indeed a high destiny, and has fine issues, for it is the function of solitude, as Thomson tells us, to 'warn the favoured soul' and to 'prompt the poet.' Poems on the subject, frequently the vehicle of satiric or moral reflections, as in Cowper's dull 'Retirement,' extend straight across the century. Goldsmith, in *The Citizen of the World*, made his Chinese philosopher descend at dead of night into the deserted streets of London there to reflect upon the transitory nature of earthly grandeur, in a fashion perfectly harmonious with the spirit of Wilson's picture:

What a gloom hangs all around. The dying lamp feebly emits a yellow gleam; no sound is heard but of the chiming clock, or the distant watchdog. All the bustle of human pride is forgotten; an hour like this may well display the emptiness of human vanity.

There will come a time, when this temporary solitude may be made continual, and the city itself, like its inhabitants, fade away, and leave a desert in its room.

What cities as great as this have once triumphed in existence, had their victories as great, joy as just, and as unbounded; and, with short-sighted presumption, promised themselves immortality. Posterity can hardly trace the situation of some; the sorrowful traveller wanders over the awful ruins of others; and, as he beholds, he learns wisdom, and feels the transcience of every sublunary possession.

'Here,' he cries, 'stood their citadel, now grown over with weeds; there their senate-house, but now the haunt of every noxious reptile; temples and theatres stood here, now only an undistinguished heap of ruin.' [2]

---

[1] Thomson's *Seasons*, edited by J. Logie Robertson, 'Summer,' lines 516 ff.

[2] Letter 117; it had already appeared in the fourth issue of Goldsmith's *Bee*, on October 27, 1759, where it is entitled, 'A City Night-Piece,' and has the motto, 'Ille dolet vere qui sine teste dolet.' In the first edition of *The Citizen of the World*, it is Letter 114, but does not include the final paragraph of the essay as printed in *The Bee*.

WILSON.   SOLITUDE

From an engraving by William Woollett, 1778

Such were Goldsmith's 'night-thoughts' in 1761, the very year in which Wilson's 'Solitude' was painted. As the century drew on-ward, emotions such as these were carefully cultivated, and the sentimentally-inclined delighted in the 'melancholy repose of a ruin' because it filled the imagination with awful images, and the young heroines of the later Gothic fiction [1] are at their best in the fitful moonlight streaming through the oriel windows of a half-ruined castle, whose turrets seem to nod under the scudding clouds. But the subject had also its profounder phase; and at last phi-losophy and romantic impulse merged into the dazzling poetry of Shelley's *Alastor* and the milder radiance of Wordsworth's *Excursion*.

The more savage side of Italian landscape, as well as the gentle Claudian one, appears on Wilson's canvas, and is, on the whole, to be deplored. Judged by his paintings, his was a serene spirit, and violence and melodrama seem out of place in his peaceful world. Nevertheless, on occasion, and probably in response to a public demand, expressed through the publishers of engravings, he did adopt the stormy and passionate manner, [2] though never the full brutality of Salvator. The most famous example in this kind — a subject selected in an unhappy moment — is 'Niobe,' [3] a land-scape painted for the Duke of Bridgewater, while Wilson was in Rome. It was a conventional subject, probably suggested by Gaspar Poussin's 'Niobe' (now at Dulwich), a typical Italian landscape, with the god and goddess shooting their shafts from the clouds, as in Wilson's picture. A repetition of 'Niobe' is now in the Tate Gallery. It illustrates the risk to a landscape of the animated figures in it. The spectator inevitably forgets the scenic back-ground in his desire to know what is going on, and how this strange situation was brought about. The Duke who had com-missioned the picture is said to have been displeased with the figures, and to have had them repainted by another hand. But a worse insult than this was the attack of Sir Joshua himself in his fourteenth discourse before the Royal Academy, delivered six

---

[1] They are delightfully described in Dr. Warren H. Smith's *Architecture in English Fiction*, New Haven, 1934.

[2] A convention illustrated in Nicholas Poussin's 'The Deluge,' Gaspar Poussin's 'The Hurricane,' and Joseph Vernet's 'La Grande Tempête.'

[3] The original drawing for the figure of Niobe is reproduced by Archer in his *Studies and Designs of Richard Wilson*, Oxford, 1811.

WILSON. NIOBE

From an engraving by William Woollett, 1761

years after Wilson's death (1788). During his lifetime, one could hardly have uttered such a criticism with impunity, for Wilson had a sharp wit and a gift of repartee. For sheer appropriateness and deadly effect, it would be difficult to find a more brilliant *mot* than Wilson's retort to a slight administered to him by Reynolds at a dinner of the Royal Academy, when the President is said to have toasted Gainsborough as the greatest living landscape-painter (a compliment not unmingled with innuendo), and Wilson cried out, 'And the greatest portrait-painter also.' Perhaps this shaft still rankled in the presidential breast. Be this as it may, the *Discourses* preserve for all time his ungenerous critique of 'Niobe':

Our late ingenious Academician, Wilson, has, I fear, been guilty, like many of his predecessors, of introducing gods and goddesses, ideal beings, into scenes which were by no means prepared to receive such personages. His landscapes were in reality too near common nature to admit super-natural objects. In consequence of this mistake, in a very admirable picture of a storm which I have seen of his hand, many figures are intro-duced in the foreground, some in apparent distress, and some struck dead, as a spectator would naturally suppose, by the lightning; had not the painter injudiciously (as I think) rather chosen that their death should be imputed to a little Apollo, who appears in the sky, with his bent bow, and that those figures should be considered as the children of Niobe. . . .

In the picture alluded to, the first idea that presents itself is that of wonder at seeing a figure in so uncommon a situation as that in which the Apollo is placed; for the clouds on which he kneels have not the appearance of being able to support him; they have neither the substance nor the form fit for the receptacle of a human figure; and they do not possess in any respect that romantic character which is appropriated to such an object, and which alone can harmonise with poetical stories.

When Sir Joshua wrote these words the paint was still wet on his portrait of Mrs. Billington, standing on a cloud, surrounded by *putti*, and holding in her hands a sheet of music, as though she were about to burst into song.[1] Had he not, in earlier days, exalted a score of ambitious society ladies to the heavens, and equipped them with various celestial trappings? Can it be that he thought these models to possess 'that romantic character' appropriate to life among the clouds?

[1] The portrait, finished in 1787, is now in the New York Public Library. Mrs. Billington was a well-known singer of the day.

But we must not exonerate Wilson by laughing at Sir Joshua, for 'Niobe' is not without very conspicuous faults, which inhere in the very nature of narrative painting. No spectator can refrain from trying to make out the dreadful events represented in the picture. A careful count, for example, discovers but thirteen of Niobe's children. Where is the missing fourteenth child? Is it conceivable that the lightning which strikes the mountain-side is to be thought of as destroying this one,— a huntsman, possibly, in the woods upon its slope? In considering such matters, our attention is distracted from something much more important — the landscape, in which, we may assume, the artist desired to express, no less than in the human figures, the horror of the scene. It is a typically Italian landscape, in which storm and convulsion have supplanted the conventional serenity. It is, as it were, a Claudian scene blasted in sudden ruin, with emphasis upon the lightning flash, the shattered cliff, the blazing castle in the middle distance, the frowning heavens, and the tree, split by a thunderbolt, still bearing all its foliage upon its prostrate boughs. Such melodrama seems more appropriate to Salvator than to the gentle Wilson; but the picture attained a certain popularity, and was several times 'repeated' by the artist.

Another picture in the same manner is 'Celadon and Amelia,' engraved by Woollett in 1766. It illustrates an incident in James Thomson's 'Summer.' [1] The number of persons destroyed by the storm is here reduced to one, but the ruined landscape is much the same, with a thunder-shattered tree, a blazing castle and a broken bridge. Below the print of the picture are the poet's words:

> The tempest caught them on the tender walk . . .
> From his void embrace,
> Mysterious Heaven, that moment to the ground,
> A blackened corse, was struck the beauteous maid.
> But who can paint the lover as he stood,
> Pierc'd by severe amazement, hating life,
> Speechless and fix'd in all the death of woe!

---

[1] 'Summer,' lines 1191 ff. In the omitted lines the lover has attempted to calm the lady's fear of the lightning:

> He, who yon skies involves
> In frowns of darkness, ever smiles on thee.

WILSON. CELADON AND AMELIA

From an engraving by William Woollett, 1766

Other pictures of the sort are 'Meleager and Atalanta,' 'Phaeton,' 'Ceyx and Alcyone,' all with landscapes more or less Salvatorian, and with human figures more or less negligible. In their engraved form they must once have been popular, and it is possible that some of the pictures were painted to supply the demand of the print-shops for engravings; but it is difficult to conceive of Wilson as having had much pleasure in them. He never delighted in the tempest as did the poet who apostrophised the night,

> Let me be
> A sharer in thy fierce and far delight,
> A portion of the tempest and of thee;

or he who, in language yet more passionate, addressed the west wind:

> Be thou, spirit fierce,
> My spirit. Be thou me, impetuous one.

Storms in Wilson's pictures are never, as in Turner's, romantic and glorious, but only catastrophic. The painter was troubled by no such turbulent passions as required a release in violent convulsions of the elements.

But Wilson has another manner in which the romance of the wild and remote unites in perfect harmony with the placid and familiar. His landscapes representing scenes in the west of England and in his native Wales, which infuse into the picturesque the charm of personal acquaintance, are perhaps his noblest works. One of the best is the painting of Mount Snowdon, now in the Castle Museum at Nottingham, engraved in 1775 by Woollett. Snowdon, the highest peak in England or Wales, called the 'king of mountains' by Mason in *Caractacus*, was made by Gray the scene of his ode, 'The Bard,' printed in 1757. Upon an inaccessible rock on the shaggy slope of the mountain, the poet places the vengeful minstrel who prophesies the doom of King Edward, who, at the head of his English army, is marching past below. After uttering his fateful curse upon the destroyer of the Welsh bards, and before leaping to death in the torrent at the base of the cliff, the passionate singer beholds visions of glory,

> solemn scenes on Snowdon's height
> Descending slow their glittering skirts unroll.

He sees, in majestic panorama, the future glory of Great Britain.

In Gray's description of mountain-scenery there is more than poetic ecstasy. From his youth up, he had been a devotee of mountains, and had associated them in imagination with the supernatural. As early as 1739, in his twenty-third year, his ascent to the Grande Chartreuse had acquainted him with scenes which he declared to be 'pregnant with religion and poetry.' This, as every historian of the Romantic Movement has pointed out, summarises the new attitude to mountain-scenery. 'One need not,' he writes, 'have a very fantastic imagination to see spirits there at noonday,' and adds — precocious youth — words suitable to the melodramatic landscapes of which mention has just been made: 'You have Death perpetually before your eyes, only so far removed, as to compose the mind without frighting it.' [1]

In a letter written at the height of Wilson's activity as a landscape-painter, Gray remarked, to his friend Palgrave, who was travelling in Scotland,[2]

I do not know how to make you amends, having neither rock, ruin, or precipice near me to send you; they do not grow in the south. . . . I congratulate you on your new acquaintance with the *savage*, the *rude* and the *tremendous*. Pray, tell me, is it anything like what you had read in your book or seen in two-shilling prints?

Mr. Palgrave's acquaintance with romantic scenery had been derived, one infers, not from nature, but from poetry, guide-books, and engravings.

More impressive perhaps, certainly more romantic, is Wilson's painting of the tarn at the summit of 'Cader Idris,' or Chair of Idris the Giant.[3] On the south side of the summit it is but a short walk from the cairn to this magnificent pool, lying calm among its embracing cliffs. The painting was exhibited at the Royal Acad-

---

[1] *Letters*, ed. Toynbee and Whibley, vol. I, p. 128, November 16, 1739.

[2] *Ib.*, vol. II, p. 586, September 6, 1758.

[3] It was shown at the British Exhibition at Burlington House in 1934, and again at Amsterdam in 1936. In the latter place, five of Wilson's pictures adequately revealed the solid base upon which his reputation as a painter reposes: the 'Villa Borghese,' a view of Lake Nemi, a British river-scene, and a country estate in Cheshire.

WILSON. MOUNT SNOWDON

From an engraving by William Woollett, 1778

emy in 1774. It might well illustrate lines destined to be famous, but which were, as yet, unwritten:

> It was a cove, a huge recess,
> That keeps till June December's snow;
> A lofty precipice in front,
> A silent tarn below. . . .

> There sometimes doth a leaping fish
> Send through the tarn a lonely cheer;
> The crags repeat the raven's croak,
> In symphony austere;
> Thither the rainbow comes — the cloud —
> And mists that spread the flying shroud;
> And sunbeams; and the sounding blast,
> That, if it could, would hurry past;
> But that enormous barrier binds it fast.

The verses are not more instinct with the spirit of romanticism than is the eighteenth century landscape.

The river-scenes painted by Wilson preserve the note of calm which is felt even in the picture of Cader Idris. In a landscape usually referred to as 'The Thames near Twickenham,' a lovely picture recently added to the National Gallery, the familiar stream is shown winding placidly between its banks, bearing upon its bosom a barge with idly-hanging sails and smoke curling upwards from the deck. The day is declining, and below the shelving banks of the stream two horses and a rider are seen, returning from labour. Two youths in the foreground emphasise the restful spirit of the scene: one leans against a tree, as if to gaze upon the glassy surface of the stream before plunging in. Although the scene is English, the tone is that of Wilson's earlier Italian pictures. Here we find once more that pervasive serenity which is commonly associated with his name.

There were features of the English landscape which failed to interest him. He gave no attention to the English woods, dear to the heart of Gainsborough, nor did he paint the English climate, as did Constable. Unlike George Morland, who has an animal's love of a thicket, Wilson enjoys the openness and sweep of a prospect, as did Claude before him. It was this very breadth and

WILSON.   SUMMIT OF CADER IDRIS

From the painting in the possession of Sir Edward Marsh

WILSON.   THE THAMES NEAR TWICKENHAM
From the picture in the National Gallery, London

openness that he himself admired in Claude. 'Why Sir,' he is said to have remarked to William Beechey, 'you may walk in Claude's pictures, and count the miles.' [1] This spaciousness — a sense of distance extending to far horizons — must, one supposes, be the most difficult of all landscape features to indicate on canvas. For this and similar qualities Wilson sacrifices all the lesser devices of landscape-painters. Save in the melodramatic pictures, painted perhaps at the instance of others, and in which the human figures are not always his own, he makes no use of sentiment, narrative, or supernatural appeal — no clap-trap of any sort. He makes no concessions to the public, and gives his admirers nothing to talk about. There is only the picture to enjoy. It would be difficult to mention a painter who more aptly illustrates the phrase, 'economy of means.' Cool and austere, he wastes no effort, follows no fashions, and makes no cheap or transitory appeal. Unlike Turner, he is never wanting in common sense; unlike Morland, he never lacks dignity or worth. One cares for the soul and centre of his work, or one can make nothing of it.

[1] M. H. Grant, *Old English Landscape Painters*, vol. I, p. 56.

VII

J. M. W. TURNER: VISION

IN any modern estimate of Turner's genius it is natural to fix attention on his water-colours, which have maintained a reputation undimmed by the passage of time; but to understand his original intentions and to recover the history of his reputation it is essential to study those pictures which he himself exhibited before the Royal Academy as the proofs of his power. When we look at his oil paintings, we follow him into a world of legend to which he gave his early allegiance and to which he never wearied of returning. But it is not that realm of light to which his work in water-colour is dedicated. The exhibited canvases, particularly those painted after the *Liber Studiorum*, plunge us into dreams, apart from the dull and commonplace scene in which we pass our mean existence. There are mystery and tragedy, for ever intruding. Despite the fact that he painted all the rivers, harbours, shipping, cathedrals, castles, mountains, ruins, and crags of the British Isles, of northern France, of Belgium, and the Rhine, and though he made all the great cities of Italy in a peculiar sense his own, his is no familiar scene, such as is known to the traveller in search of the picturesque. It is, rather, a ruined Paradise, in which, amid beauties innumerable, we encounter all manner of catastrophic disturbance, conflagration, avalanche, earthquake, shipwreck, hurricane, and warfare, with Death stalking through the mountain-passes, and pacing in fury upon the sea. The melodrama of Salvator himself is not more intense than that of Turner. In spite of his paltry painting of the human figure, there is a grandeur in his rendering of the works of man, who, undefeated by the perils of the desert and the sea, rears his towers to the sky, 'pinnacled dim in the intense inane.' There is evidence all about us of some invisible but Titanic conflict, a war of gods and evil ones, a struggle in which man is somehow involved, though he is powerless to comprehend its cause or to foresee the destiny towards which he is driven.

In history, no less than in legend, upon the quiet plains of Italy

TURNER. BERRY POMEROY CASTLE

From the *Liber Studiorum*

and in the stormy passes of the Alps, in the repose of Nature as in
its frenzy, we see this strange juxtaposition — man in his majestic
strength and his pitiable weakness, set in the midst of a world at
once calm and treacherous, terrible and beautiful. Even in pictures of actual historical events, 'The Battle of Trafalgar' and
'The Field of Waterloo,' there is already something of a legendary
nature. The historic has begun to fade, mystery to invade the
scene.

Imagination dominates, even when he is drawing an actual
building; so that it has in truth been possible to discuss whether
Plate 58 in the *Liber Studiorum* represents Raglan Castle (in Mon-
mouthshire) or, more probably, Berry Pomeroy (in Devonshire).
The one thing about which there can be no discussion is that it
is an 'Enchanted Castle,' like one of Claude's, or the castle dimly
discerned in Plate 53, called 'Solitude.' [1] Ruskin told Mr. Rawlinson, the editor of the *Liber*, that at Raglan 'legends of gray
knights and enchanted ladies kept the woodman's children away at
sunset.' [2]

The exhibited canvases are frequently laden with what is now
cheaply called a 'message,' which can seldom be put into words,
though Turner habitually makes the attempt. His use of language
was often childish, and his titles, like Wordsworth's, are often
annoyingly long and detailed. He uses a great many words to
explain his dream, but they only serve to tarnish it. Carthage, for
example, is to him not merely an antique city, or even a dream,
but a symbol. The picture of its decline, exhibited in 1817,[3] in
Turner's forty-second year, was accompanied by this elaborate
explanation:

The Decline of the Carthaginian Empire. Rome, being determined
on the overthrow of her hated rival, demanded from her such terms as
might either force her into war, or ruin her by compliance; the enervated
Carthaginians, in their anxiety for peace, consented to give up even their
arms and their children.

[1] Turner's startling indifference to mere fact is shown in the successive states of his
engraving of Eton College Chapel (*Liber Studiorum*, Plate 79, 'Ploughing, Eton'), where
the number of windows is altered from eight to six. Rawlinson, p. 181.

[2] Rawlinson, p. 140.

[3] The only picture which he exhibited that year.

TURNER. DECLINE OF CARTHAGE

From an engraving by J. B. Allen

Verses follow:

> At Hope's delusive smile,
> The chieftain's safety and the mother's pride
> Were to th' insidious conqueror's grasp resign'd;
> While o'er the western wave th' ensanguined sun,
> In gathering haze, a stormy signal spread,
> And set portentous.

The spectator is not trusted to discover the full meaning for himself. In the foreground are the emblems of self-indulgence, the vice which has brought about the surrender of the Carthaginian arms and the Carthaginian children. The city is desolate; the cry of the bereaved mother is heard in its streets. So far it is easy to go without assistance from the painter. But what was the significance of the lesson in 1817? It seems a strange sermon to preach to England in the year of her triumph, just when the Napoleonic menace had been brought definitely to an end. What action the artist would urge the nation to take is not clear, and perhaps was not very clear to him. A prophetic warning of the dangers of luxury is so inadequately conveyed by landscape, anyhow, that it is easy to understand the contempt commonly displayed for Turner's pictures of this kind.

But may the scene not have a value apart from this lesson? It depicts a dream-city, like its companion-piece, far better known, called 'Dido building Carthage.' The two pictures are not so much a lesson in the dangers of luxury as a symbol of the dreams and soaring ambitions of mankind. They depict the insatiable pride which goads man to undertake tasks more and more stupendous, until at length both they and he are plunged into a common ruin. Such is the vanity of human ambitions. The quotation in verse is drawn from Turner's hypothetical poem, 'The Fallacies of Hope,'—a phrase which sums up the meaning of many of his more elaborate pictures,—from which he often pretended to quote. Turner always referred to it as a 'manuscript,' though no such work has ever been discovered among his papers. Other poems were found, but so defective in rhythm, metre, syntax, and intelligibility, that the few who have been curious enough to examine them have gained but little. They are, nevertheless, of some significance, since a man's aspirations, even when falla-cious, furnish a key to his work. Turner insists upon literary relationships. His knowledge of poetry must have been wider than is commonly realised, for he is constantly quoting from Mil-ton, James Thomson, and Byron, to mention no others. His work as an illustrator of Rogers, Scott, and Byron must have demanded a certain amount of reading. The notion that he could have acquired the necessary information in any other way is not worth discussion.

This indebtedness to poetry is to be found in one of his most famous canvases — to Americans perhaps the most familiar of all. Its full title is 'Slavers throwing overboard the Dead and Dying — Typhon coming on,' and when shown at the exhibition of the Academy in 1840, it was accompanied by a quotation, even worse than usual, from 'The Fallacies of Hope':

> Aloft all hands, strike the topmasts and belay;
> Yon angry setting sun and fierce-edged clouds
> Declare the typhon's coming.
> Before it sweep your decks, throw overboard
> The dead and dying — ne'er heed their chains.
> Hope, Hope, fallacious Hope!
> Where is thy market now?

This picture was bought by John Ruskin's father, who pre-sented it to him on New Year's day, 1844, in token of his brilliant success as the author of *Modern Painters*. In the next instalment of that work it became the subject of a famous passage of lyrical prose,[1] in which the young essayist, speaking out of the fulness of his knowledge, declared it to be 'the noblest sea' that Turner ever painted, 'and if so, the noblest certainly ever painted by man.' But though the noblest of all sea-scapes, it was offered for sale by Ruskin, with other pictures, in 1869.[2] The subject, he explained, had become painful to him; but there was nothing painful in the ultimate acquisition of £2,042.5s. by its sale. It was brought to this

---

[1] Part II, section 5, chapter III, paragraph 39.

[2] 'The Slave-Ship' was, however, bought in, and remained in Ruskin's possession until 1872, when it was sold, apparently through the exertions of Professor Norton, and brought to America. See *Letters of Ruskin to Charles Eliot Norton*, vol. II, pp. 48–49.

TURNER. THE SLAVE-SHIP

From the painting in the Boston Museum of Fine Arts

country, and, after a few years, passed into Miss Alice Hooper's collection. But a fine to-do was caused when George Inness roundly denounced the picture as the most infernal piece of clap-trap ever painted, and asserted that its colour was harsh, disagree-able, and discordant, and that it had 'as much to do with human affections and thoughts as a ghost.' When the picture was lent to the Boston Museum in 1896, the controversy as to its merits was renewed with great ardour. The art-critic of the *Transcript* outdid Inness by suggesting that Ruskin was colour-blind, and that 'he wrote neither good English nor good art-criticism.' But the friends of the picture prevailed, and in 1899 it passed into the per-manent possession of the Museum.

So great was the controversy over the merits of Turner's man-ner that almost no attention was given to the subject-matter. Yet it seems natural to inquire what could have been the significance of exhibiting to the British public of 1840 a picture representing the cruelty of the slave-trade. A hundred years earlier it would have been timely enough. Turner, who knew the manifold life along the banks of the Thames and all the shipping on its bosom, may possibly have seen, when a boy, a vessel clearing out for slaves, before that traffic was halted, early in the nineteenth century; but he had certainly never seen a ship laden with slaves, as he had never seen a slaver or any other craft in tropic waters, struck by a typhoon.

The picture takes on a new interest when we realise that it illustrates a well-known passage in a favourite poem of Turner's, which he had probably read in boyhood. All eighteenth century readers knew Thomson's *Seasons*. If Coleridge found a dog-eared copy of it in the public room of an English inn, why should there not have been one in old Mr. Turner's barber-shop? Why should the boy Turner not have read the poem during his school-days at Brentford? Anyhow, the man, like other English painters, knew and loved the poem, and the part that he knew best was 'Summer.'

Thomson, as often, has been extolling British commerce, and dwelling on the danger of storms. He reaches a kind of climax — such, at least, as he is capable of — in his account of the 'typhon' in tropic seas:

But chief at sea, whose every flexile wave
Obeys the blast, the aerial tumult swells.
In the dread ocean, undulating wide,
Beneath the radiant line that girts the globe,
The circling Typhon, whirled from point to point,
Exhausting all the rage of all the sky,
And dire Ecnephia [1] reign . . .
                          Then down at once,
Precipitant, descends a mingled mass
Of roaring winds and flame, and rushing floods . . .
Increasing still the terrors of these storms,
His jaws horrific armed with threefold fate,
Here dwells the direful shark. Lured by the scent
Of steaming crowds, of rank disease, and death,
Behold! he rushing cuts the briny flood,
Swift as the gale can bear the ship along;
And, from the partners of that cruel trade,
Which spoils unhappy Guinea of her sons,
Demands his share of prey; demands themselves.
The stormy fates descend: one death involves
Tyrants and slaves; when straight, their mangled limbs
Crashing at once, he dyes the purple seas
With gore, and riots in the vengeful meal. [2]

Here, then, are all the familiar details of Turner's picture: the 'typhon' itself, the purple seas, the slaver, the bodies in the water, and the sharks. Turner's mad departure from fact in representing the chained legs of the slaves as floating on the water is perhaps the extreme example of his indifference to natural law when he is concerned to bring out the moral of a picture.

Another favourite poet, particularly in Turner's later life, was Lord Byron, of whose stormy emotions he seems to have had an instinctive understanding. He quoted from the third canto of *Childe Harold* (a poem given to the world less than two years before), when he exhibited in 1818 his depressing picture of the 'Field of Waterloo.' [3]

[1] Unlike 'typhon,' the word 'ecnephia,' signifying, apparently, *cloudburst*, did not establish itself in English.

[2] 'Summer,' lines 980 ff.; 1013 ff.

[3] Cf. the vignette on the title-page of the fourteenth volume of Murray's edition of Byron's works, 1832–34.

Last noon beheld them full of lusty life,
Last eve in Beauty's circle proudly gay;
The midnight brought the signal-sound of strife,
The morn, the marshalling in arms — the day,
Battle's magnificently-stern array!
The thunder-clouds close o'er it, which when rent,
The earth is covered thick with other clay,
Which her own clay shall cover, heaped and pent,
Rider and horse, friend, foe, in one red burial blent!

When Turner made use of these lines he was already known as an artist who had derived frequent inspiration from the Continent; but he had not yet seen Italy. His first visit to that country was paid in 1819, and from that time onward his name was ever more and more intimately associated with it. In a happy hour he was asked to furnish vignette-engravings to a new edition of the poems of Samuel Rogers, the 'banker-poet,' who had published in 1823, shortly before the death of Lord Byron, a series of poems on Italy. These blank-verse meditations had no success. How could Rogers have hoped to succeed when Byron had, as it were, appropriated the subject, and captivated the English public with the fourth canto of *Childe Harold*? But there was another way for a wealthy man to succeed in descriptive poetry. Rogers arranged for the publication of a sumptuous edition, with illustrations by Turner, Stothard, and others. The twenty-four steel-engraved vignettes supplied by Turner, seldom more than three inches high, seem, when closely examined, as lovely in detail as one of his heroic canvases, and they made the book famous at once. It was natural, therefore, that similar illustrations should be demanded for other volumes, among them Murray's collected edition of the Works of Byron, the issue of which was begun in 1832.

In the exhibition of the Royal Academy that year Turner paid a characteristic tribute to the memory of the poet for whose works he must already have been drawing his illustrations,[1] by showing a large and glowing canvas in the Claudian manner entitled, 'Childe Harold's Pilgrimage — Italy.' To it he appended in the catalogue a quotation from the fourth canto, inaccurately given.[2]

[1] Of the twenty-six engravings of Turner, only six represent Italian scenes.
[2] Canto IV, stanza 26.

And now, fair Italy!
Thou art the garden of the world.
Even in thy desert what is like to thee?
Thy very weeds are beautiful, thy waste
More rich than other climes' fertility:
Thy wreck a glory, and thy ruin graced
With an immaculate charm which cannot be defaced.

Since the oil picture has been somewhat injured by time, and the details are not easily seen, I quote the description of Mr. C. F. Bell, who inspected it at a somewhat earlier day. 'View overlooking a broad wooded valley; in the middle distance a river flowing round a promontory, and crossed on the right by a bridge with a tower, on the left, hills, covered with trees and ruins, rise from the brink of the river; in the foreground, slightly to left, a tall stone pine, a little to right a group of figures seated on the ground, others dancing; the Pilgrim emerging from a grotto on the extreme left. Blue sky, effect of brilliant sunlight.' [1]

It was not unfrequently that Turner made the attempt, as he does in 'Childe Harold's Pilgrimage — Italy,' to pay honour to the great. In canvas after canvas he expresses, sometimes blunderingly, his respect for his predecessors and colleagues, and the pride that he feels in his profession. Thus in 1820 he exhibited 'Rome from the Vatican. Raffaelle, accompanied by La Fornarina, preparing his pictures for the decoration of the Loggia,' a strange scene, with the 'Madonna of the Chair' visible in the foreground; in 1827, 'Rembrandt's Daughter,' in which, it is said, there was formerly visible a canvas inscribed 'Rembrandt'; in 1833, 'Bridge of Sighs, Ducal Palace and Custom-house, Venice: Canaletti painting'; in 1841, 'Depositing of John Bellini's three pictures in la Chiesa Redentore, Venice.' None of these could have been painted in any conceivable rivalry with the artist represented; they represent Turner's admiration for his predecessors, his desire to claim relationship with them, and his willingness to receive inspiration from them.[2] The strangest of these paintings is a round pic-

---

[1] *Exhibited Works of Turner*, p. 118. The picture is now in the national collection.

[2] The classic instance of the painter's emulous nature is his bequest to the National Gallery of 'Dido building Carthage' and 'The Sun rising in a Mist,' on condition that they hang beside two landscapes by Claude. This was a somewhat rash stipulation, since

TURNER. CHILDE HAROLD'S PILGRIMAGE

From an engraving by J. T. Willmore

ture entitled 'Bacchus and Ariadne' (exhibited in 1840), in which the two leading figures and the little faun are taken directly from Titian's famous canvas in the National Gallery. Turner's figures are as usual badly drawn, but the picture is redeemed by the long prospect down the river, on the right, the glowing sky, the Italian pine, and the dream-city crowning the hillside on the left. As paintings, all these are perhaps without high merit, but as examples of Turner's pleasant, though eccentric, intentions, they deserve not to be forgotten.

His relation with English painters is no less remarkable. In 1822, he conceived a plan (never carried out) of issuing four engravings from pictures of his own in rivalry with four of Wilson's melodramatic plates, 'Niobe,' 'Ceyx,' 'Cyledon,' and 'Phaeton' (as Turner called them). In a letter addressed to a publisher proposing the scheme, he speaks with high respect of Wilson and his engraver, Woollett, as powerful antagonists. 'If we fall, we fall by contending with giant strength,' wrote Turner. 'This,' Mr. Hamerton remarked long ago, 'is clear evidence that, when quite in his maturity, Turner looked up to Wilson instead of considering him an inferior, and that his own project of contending against him was accompanied by certain misgivings.'

Turner's indebtedness extends even to his contemporaries; his famous canvas called 'The Frosty Morning,' which Colonel Grant considers to be his masterpiece, seems to have been painted in rivalry with John Crome, that austere and modest painter of open air and light. For such influence (if it existed) we can but be grateful. Even earlier than this, he seems to have painted deliberately

---

certain competent judges prefer the tranquil art of Claude to the spectacular style of Turner. I cannot but believe, for my part, that even if Turner intended thus to enter into rivalry with Claude and demonstrate his superiority, he meant also to acknowledge his indebtedness.

Much the same thing must be true of the relation of the *Liber Studiorum* to Claude's *Liber Veritatis*. Turner must have known that, though his own 'book' was of a more grandiose character, intended, as Mr. Rawlinson has said, 'to illustrate his whole range of powers,' it betrayed in almost every plate his indebtedness to earlier masters. Contempt for Claude (such as Ruskin expressed in *Modern Painters*) I do not find there, nor can I believe that Turner put it there. There is a kind of parallel in Dryden's 'imitations' of Chaucer, which show affection for a classic work and indebtedness to it at the very moment when they betray a failure really to understand it.

in the manner of David Wilkie. It was in 1807 that he exhibited a genre-picture with the confusing title, 'A country blacksmith disputing upon the price of iron and the price charged to the butcher for shoeing his poney,' which, like 'The Straw Yard' (Plate 7 in the *Liber Studiorum*) is an unsuccessful experiment in another man's field. Sir David Wilkie, an exact contemporary of Turner and a Royal Academician, long thought of as one of the more eminent painters of Great Britain, has suffered in reputation, owing to the decline of genre-painting, which has been fatally connected with pictures existing primarily to tell a story. Turner lacks the humour and the intelligibility which mark Wilkie's best work, and the picture of the blacksmith, which is much darkened, is interesting to-day as emphasising the fact that Turner's so-called rivalry with a contemporary painter implied no real or lasting antagonism.

To Wilkie Turner paid the finest of all these tributes, a picture often called 'The Burial of Wilkie,' though more correctly known as 'Peace — Burial at Sea.' On his return from the Holy Land, Wilkie had become critically ill, and had died on board the *Oriental* at Gibraltar. He was buried at sea, beyond the straits, in June, 1841. Turner's painting was shown at the next exhibition of the Academy, and the reference in the catalogue was accompanied by a quotation from *The Fallacies of Hope*:

> The midnight torch gleamed o'er the steamer's side,
> And Merit's corse was yielded to the tide.

A large ship, with black smoke issuing from its funnel and its sails black against the sky, dominates the scene. Amidships is a blaze of light from the funeral torches, as an almost invisible coffin is lowered into the sea.

This painting, which has retained its popularity with the British public, was completed in the artist's sixty-seventh year, but though age was closing down upon him, he had lost none of his characteristic audacity. The scene which he chose to depict, he could of course have known only from hearsay; but another artist, even though obliged to rely wholly upon his imagination, would have made an effort to be as nearly realistic as possible. Not so Turner. Since he desired to have the Rock of Gibraltar as a background, he boldly represented the ship as in Mediterranean waters and as nearer land than it would have been on the occasion of a sea-burial. Moreover, he gave the shore, as it were, a part in the obsequies; for in the picture we were originally meant to see signal lights ashore — indeed even a rising rocket — the whole scene reflected in the tranquil waters, and the light of a new moon visible in the sky, to the right. The emotion of the painter is expressed in these inanimate details, as in the drifting smoke and the black sails.[1]

A steamboat in the centre of a picture intended as a kind of elegy must have seemed novel enough in 1842; but it was highly characteristic of Turner, who loved to watch the smoke melting away into the mists of the sea. In the popular picture of the 'Fighting Téméraire, tugged to its Last Berth,' another elegy (exhibited in 1839), the most prominent object is the ugly tug-boat, with its belching smoke-stack.[2]

Turner's dramatisation of the sea, as it has been called, is probably the fullest and most varied known to marine painting; and, as in the making of a play, that which the dramatist himself has not experienced, he has imagined. Turner, we may safely assume, had never been on a whaling expedition, and had never seen a whale; but he took great delight in imagining and bodying forth on canvas the life which he could so easily infer from what he had read. Four pictures representing whale-ships were exhibited in 1845-46, which, as Turner himself disclosed, are derived from a book,

[1] He paid a tribute to the memory of Sir Thomas Lawrence in his water-colour sketch 'from memory,' showing the funeral cortège moving up the steps of St. Paul's Cathedral. It was exhibited by the Academy in the year of Lawrence's death, 1830. The picture is now in the British Museum.

[2] Turner's depiction of tugs and steamboats is particularly noticeable in his *Rivers of France*; see 'Paris,' 'Confluence of the Seine and Marne,' 'Melun,' 'Havre,' 'Caudebec,' and 'Between Quilleboeuf and Villequier.' The last suggests the arrangement afterwards used in the 'Fighting Téméraire.'

Contemporary with the 'Burial of Wilkie' is another painting of a steamboat — shown in the Academy's same exhibition — under the title, 'Snow storm — steamboat off a harbour's mouth making signals in shallow water, and going by the lead. The author was in this storm on the night the Ariel left Harwich.' Whatever be the truth about Turner's experiences during this storm, the picture of it is admirable: smoke, signal lights, fog, and breaking waves are all mingled in one element which has enwrapped the world.

The picture is in the Tate Gallery.

TURNER.   PEACE — BURIAL AT SEA

From an engraving by J. Cousen

Thomas Beale's *Natural History of the Sperm-Whale* (1838; second edition, 1839), a readable book, respectfully mentioned by Melville in *Moby-Dick*. It contains a few simple woodcuts which must have been useful to Turner in various ways. The picture in the Metropolitan Museum reveals the detail, derived from Beale, of the boats put out to dispatch the creature. Mrs. Homans's picture, now in the Fogg Museum, belonging to the same series, is perhaps an earlier study. The smaller boats are not visible; but, as in the Metropolitan example, the great ship herself is visible through the mists — a dreamlike thing, with a touch of mystery about her.

This sense of mystery —'of the old sea some reverential fear'— is usually present in Turner, and in many of his pictures he crosses into the realm of the supernatural. In the famous story-picture of 'Ulysses deriding Polyphemus' (1829), a group of nymphs hold globes of light above the surface of the sea, as though to guide the ship upon her way. A similar device is used in a later picture belonging to the period here discussed, 'The Parting of Hero and Leander' (1837).[1] The palace, the terraces, and the treacherous Hellespont, with its tossing waves, display Turner's old fondness for dream-cities and stormy seas, here somewhat rashly united. The great wave on the right breaks into a foam of sea-nymphs who seem to warn the lover of his danger. And here once more he depicted in the mounting waves, the scudding clouds, and the moon half hidden in mist the splendour, the passion, and the turbulence of love.

This is one of many late pictures which it is hard to praise, and, indeed, little praise has been given it. Mr. Monkhouse goes so far as to say that it 'bears some traces . . . of failing powers both of mind and body,' but this seems an odd assertion regarding a picture painted before 'The Fighting Téméraire,' 'The Slave-Ship,' 'Rockets and Blue Lights,' and 'The Burial of Wilkie.' The fact, whether we like it or not, is that Turner, during half a century of continuous activity, never wavered in his devotion to this kind of painting. It represented his 'grand manner,' derived from the great masters, and on his achievement in such work he expected

[1] In the Tate Gallery.

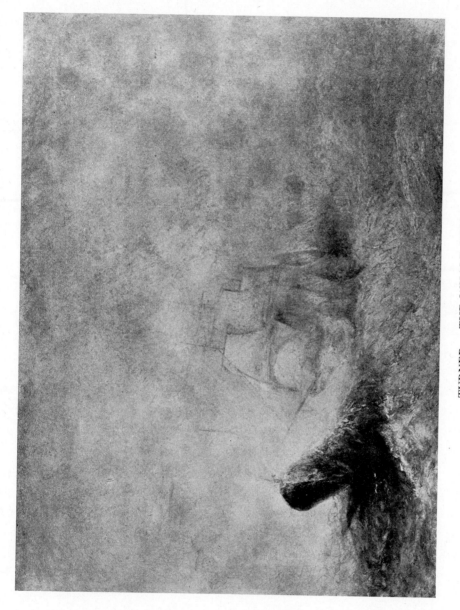

TURNER. THE WHALE-SHIP

From the painting in the possession of Mrs. Robert Homans

TURNER.   THE PARTING OF HERO AND LEANDER

From an engraving by S. Bradshaw

his reputation largely to repose. He therefore kept up his exhibitions of such canvases to the end. He showed his last works at the Academy in 1850, the year before his death. There were four of them, all belonging to the Carthaginian series which he had begun thirty-eight years before.[1]

[1] Three of them were catalogued with quotations from *The Fallacies of Hope*; all were retained in the artist's own collection, and became the property of the nation.

VIII

CONSTABLE: REVERENCE

THE contrast between Turner and Constable, like that between Reynolds and Gainsborough, or Tennyson and Browning, is inevitable. The two were of an age: Turner born in 1775, Constable in 1776; the one a product of the metropolis, born in Drury Lane, the son of a barber; the other a country boy, born in a remote village in Suffolk, where his father owned mills at Dedham and Flatford, along the banks of the placid Stour. For the quiet world of his boyhood Constable had through life an abiding passion, and felt no gipsy temptation to wander over the world in search of the picturesque. Wherever he went, he found beauty all about him. Later he lived in or near London, as an ambitious painter must needs do, but never left England, even for Scotland or Wales. Before his marriage, he did, to be sure, visit Derbyshire (1801) and the Lake District, and in both places painted certain typical scenes such as Mam Tor, Langdale, Helvellyn, and the Lakes; but, as was noticed long ago, these he never used for any large picture. Nor had he that romantic delight in mountains characteristic of Turner and the poets; the 'power of hills' never descended upon him; and Leslie records that he heard him say that 'the solitude of mountains oppressed his spirits.' The stormy paths of open sea never lured him to communion; his most important voyage to sea appears to have been a trip from London to Deal — an exploit of his earlier manhood. His marine pictures, beautiful as they are, show chiefly such a knowledge of the sea as may be gained from the shore. He never cared for 'sights.' His home-keeping nature is indicated by his attitude to Italy. He loved it as the inspiration of Wilson and Claude, and copied the Italian landscapes of the latter with devoted ardour. Of the 'Narcissus' in Sir George Beaumont's collection he wrote to his wife: 'How enchanting and lovely it is; far, very far surpassing any other landscape I ever beheld.' Yet he could be content never to see Italy, since he was born 'to paint a happier land.'

Turner was a celibate and an eccentric, who followed his impulses, and kept the public from his doors by sheer ferocity, for he knew that a painter, when driven by the creative goad, must hide from the distractions of society. But Constable, a devoted husband and father, could not remain long in solitude, and experienced, therefore, the torture of two conflicting passions, one impelling him to a normal domesticity, with its thousand distracting cares, and the other scourging him to the joy and terror of creative activity. As a married man, with seven children, he was destined to be a somewhat harried, though human and lovable being.

Again, the recognition for which Constable had long to wait had come at once to Turner, and had enabled the barber's son to devote himself whole-heartedly to painting and the search for inspiration. He became an Associate of the Academy at the age of twenty-seven, and was received into full membership three years later; whereas Constable, who became an Associate only at forty-three, was kept waiting ten years more for full membership, which was, even after such delay, somewhat grudgingly conceded. This deferred recognition was the harder to bear, since it was an era when Academy approval stimulated the demand for one's pictures, and Constable's quiet landscapes had excited little attention. At the age of thirty-eight he had sold none, and, indeed, in all his life of sixty-one years he had no startling success in England, though he was permitted to realise that his influence in Paris had been noteworthy. But Continental approval meant less to him than it commonly does to other painters.

The universal attention so easily won by his brilliant rival must have been galling to watch, but it never embittered Constable. Though it required an effort of will to be fair to so spectacular a genius as Turner's, he was adequate to the task. There are phrases in Constable's letters that may be taken for starts of envy, as when he speaks of 'bravura' as the vice of painters —'an attempt at something beyond the truth'— and his reference to Turner's 'violence to all natural feeling'; but, allowing for such just criticisms, Constable is more than fair, and his praise of Turner's exhibited canvases is beyond what would be bestowed to-day. Of 'The Bay of Baiae, with Apollo and the Sibyl,' he says, 'Turner is stark mad with ability'; and, later, in 1836, 'Turner has outdone himself; he seems to paint with tinted steam, so evanescent and so airy.' There are moments of course when he expressed a not unnatural pride in being 'independent of him who would be lord over all — I mean Turner,' but he never really stints his praise. 'Turner,' he wrote in 1829, 'has some golden visions, glorious and beautiful; but they are only visions, still they are art, and one could live and die with *such* pictures in one's house.' He once remarked in a letter to Leslie:

I am much interested with your account of the pictures at Petworth. I remember most of Turner's early works; amongst them was one of singular intricacy and beauty; it was a canal with numerous boats making thousands of beautiful shapes, and I think the most complete work of genius I ever saw.

If this be not generosity, where is generosity to be found?

But admiration implied no subservience. Constable knew that his own ability was of a totally different sort. He loved to pass his time in familiar scenes, close to the green turf, noting the effect of wandering breezes on the foliage, and attempting to sketch the scudding clouds overhead —'skying,' as he called it. How simple is the catalogue of his interests, concentrated in the fields where his mind is at its most calm and comfortable, and where the bursting spring reminds him of the Saviour's resurrection. He delights in the sound of water escaping from mill-dams, in willows, old rotten planks, slimy posts and brickwork, sheep-cotes, sodden timber-props, water-plants, willow stumps, sedges, and old nets; and ever, again and again, the sky, 'very bright and fresh, gray clouds running fast,' when it seems to be almost merged with the earth, enveloping it in a soft warm mist, breaking down in sudden showers, which pass onward with an equal suddenness — light, dews, breezes, bloom, and freshness. If one can be happy amid such things, if they afford sufficient inspiration, so that one is not obliged to go in search of picturesque subjects, but may find beauty at his very door, where the familiar puts on an air of novelty with every day and with every changing hour, how fortunate may one count oneself! When Constable speaks of his 'limited and abstracted art,' which is to be found 'under every hedge and in every lane,' we realise that upon him has been bestowed one of the greatest blessings that a man may possess — a reverence for familiar things and a tendency to value them in proportion to their nearness. Here is a source of contentment which all the hubbub and confusion of the world and all the manifold distractions of the daily life cannot take away. It is the great quality of the Dutch School. It enabled Constable to paint contentedly at East Bergholt, at Hampstead, at Salisbury, at Brighton — wherever the current of life might carry him. So he fulfilled what he conceived to be the duty of a painter, to 'make something out of nothing'; 'in attempting this,' he adds, the painter will 'almost of necessity become poetical.'

A general air of familiarity pervades the large landscape in the Huntington Gallery, 'A View on the Stour, near Dedham.' A painter who has delighted in the boys pushing the barges, the horse, the idle sails, the weeds in the foreground, the bridge in the middle distance, and the church-tower in the distance, will have no uneasy desire to seek out the picturesque, but will find it among the well-known and well-loved objects of the daily existence. Similar in manner was 'The Hay Wain,' which was one of the pictures to introduce Constable's influence into France.

It is indicative of the deep faith within him that he habitually ignored the suggestion of his friends and critics that he should display a little more variety. His favourite associate and counsellor, the Reverend John Fisher of Salisbury, once ventured to express the hope that he would 'diversify' his subject; particularly with regard to the time of day; and, quoting one of the painter's favourite poets, remarked, 'Thomson, you know, wrote not four Summers, but four "Seasons."' There are but few exceptions: one, an autumnal landscape, 'The Cenotaph' (to which reference will later be made), and another, a winter scene, called 'Gandish Cottage, East Bergholt,' depicting a house covered with snow, and, in the foreground, a frozen pond. This canvas is said to have been painted in youth for the artist's sister. It is now in the Pennsylvania Museum, and, in order that it may do no mischief to our general notions about Constable, it is kept in the vault, where nobody can see it.

To Mr. Fisher's suggestion of variety, Constable replied:

I regard all you say, but I do not enter into that notion of varying one's plans to keep the publick in good humour. Subject and change of weather and effect will always afford variety. What if Van de Velde had quited his sea-pieces, or Ruysdal his waterfalls, or Hobima his native woods. Would not the world have lost so many features in art? I know that you wish for no material alteration; but I have to combat from high quarters, even Lawrence, the seeming plausible argument that *subject* makes the picture. Perhaps you think an evening effect or a warm picture might do.[1]

Mr. Fisher sent to Constable an amusing anecdote of his little boy who had his own way of reciting the catechism:

When your pet, Belim,[2] repeats his Catechism, we cannot make him say otherwise than, 'And walk in the *same fields* all the days of my life'; he might have a worse idea of happiness.

To this Constable replied at once:

The anecdote of dear *Belim* is very pretty; depend on it, the love of nature is strongly implanted in man. . . . I have lately been into Suffolk, and have had some delightful walks 'in the *same feilds*.' Bless the dear boy! our Ideas of happiness are the same.[2]

It has often been pointed out that Constable was an admirer of William Cowper, the poet and letter-writer. The two have the same reverence for familiar scenes, undisturbed by any itching or romantic desire for novelty or change. In the first book of *The Task*,[3] Cowper describes how he and Mrs. Unwin delight to 'walk in the same fields'— how, indeed, they have walked in them, with increasing pleasure, for full twenty years. Cowper's fields, the Olney meadows sloping gently to the quiet Ouse, are at a remove from Constable's Suffolk fields; but the poet's lines read like a verbal rendering of the painter's 'View on the Stour':

> Here Ouse, slow winding through a level plain
> Of spacious meads with cattle sprinkled o'er,
> Conducts the eye along his sinuous course
> Delighted. There, fast rooted in his bank,
> Stand never overlooked, our favourite elms,
> That screen the herdsman's solitary hut;

[1] Leslie and Shirley, *Life of Constable* (1937), p. 175.
[2] Ib., p. 212. 'Belim' is the family nickname for William. The spelling and punctuation in the passages quoted are Constable's.   [3] Lines 163 ff.

CONSTABLE. THE RIVER STOUR

From the painting in the Huntington Art Gallery, San Marino, California

While far beyond, and overthwart the stream,
That, as with molten glass, inlays the vale,
The sloping land recedes into the clouds;
Displaying on its varied side the grace
Of hedge-row beauties numberless, square tower,
Tall spire, from which the sound of cheerful bells
Just undulates upon the listening ear;
Groves, heaths, and smoking villages remote.

Scenes must be beautiful which, daily viewed,
Please daily, and whose novelty survives
Long knowledge and the scrutiny of years.

Words could not more adequately embody the artistic creed of John Constable and the scenes which illustrate it.

But Cowper was not the only poet under whose influence the painter fell. Two others, one a predecessor of Cowper, the other his successor, shared Constable's affections — James Thomson and William Wordsworth. The artist himself had recourse to Thomson in describing his landscape commonly called 'The Cornfield':

April 8th. (1826) . . . I have despatched a large landscape to the Academy, upright, the size of my *Lock*, but a subject of a very different nature: inland kind of thing, corn fields, a close lane. But it is not neglected in any part; the trees are more than usually studied, the extremities well defined, as well as the stems; they are shaken by a pleasant and healthful breeze *at Noon*:

while now a fresher Gale
Sweeping with shadowy gust the feilds of corn,[1] etc.

It is a cheerful scene, and though there are but the shepherd-boy in the foreground and two workmen in the middle distance — both afterthoughts — to animate the landscape, it has no air of solitude or remoteness. We are close to the heart of England, and could never feel from home in such a place.

In one of his lectures on the history of landscape-painting, there is further explanation of his fondness for the poet Thomson. In the course of his remarks he quoted no fewer than sixteen lines, introductory to 'Winter,' as a 'beautiful instance of the poet identifying his own feelings with external nature.' If it be for the painter, as

[1] Thomson, 'Summer,' lines 1653-54.

CONSTABLE.   THE CORNFIELD
From the painting in the National Gallery, London

well as for the poet, to receive a landscape into his heart, may we
not infer that it is the spectator's function thus to receive the picture? Constable was correct in his estimate of Thomson's influence.
Thomson taught his readers to view familiar scenes with appreciation and gratitude; William Cowper in verse, and Constable in
painting are, in this regard, his successors. Thomson's lines in
'Spring' (102 ff.) read like a prophecy of Constable:

> Oft let me wander o'er the dewy fields,
> Where freshness breathes, and dash the trembling drops
> From the bent bush, as through the verdant maze
> Of sweet-briar hedges I pursue my walk;
> Or taste the smell of dairy.

As Constable had favourite fields, so he had favourite buildings.
He enjoyed such old, weather-beaten and sometimes dilapidated
structures as seem almost to have grown into harmonious relationship with their rustic environment — sheds, bridges, locks, Willy
Lott's cottage, the Glebe Farm, and, above all, wind-mills and
water-mills. Constable had been a miller in youth, and the love of
the crossed sails and dripping wheels never left him, for they sent
his memory back to his boyhood, and turned his eyes to rippling
streams and to the ever-changing sky.

To buildings of a more stately kind he was by no means indifferent. He followed the fashion of the day by painting country-
houses and baronial halls, parish churches, castles, and even ruins.
But his choice among all such buildings is Salisbury Cathedral, his
familiarity with which was the result of his friendship with the
Reverend John Fisher, a member of the cathedral chapter, a life-
long admirer and advocate, who encouraged him, bought his pictures, and believed in him through years of neglect by the public.

In contrast to Turner, who painted every cathedral and ruined
abbey that he could come at, Constable was content simply to
return to Salisbury again and again,[1] until he knew its infinite
variety, with the sunshine lighting up every buttress and pinnacle,
and its spire, slender as a maiden, seen through a natural Gothic

---

[1] There are also pencil-sketches of Chichester and Worcester Cathedrals, but they
were never made the subject of easel-pictures.

CONSTABLE.   SALISBURY CATHEDRAL FROM THE BISHOP'S GARDEN

From the painting in the Frick Collection

arch of trees. Turner's painting of 'Salisbury from the Cloisters' [1]
shows the tower and crossing viewed through a trefoil opening in a
cloister-arch — a spectacular effect. But when Constable seeks
variety of treatment, he draws the church in association with his
favourite fields. In all such pictures we see his ability to find beauty
in commonplace and ugly things, in stumps of trees, water-soaked
timbers, weeds, flat-bottomed boats and barges, cart-horses, and
what not. 'No, Madam, there is nothing ugly,' he is said to have
remarked to a lady who, looking at an engraving, called it an ugly
thing, 'I never saw an ugly thing in my life; for let the form of an
object be what it may, light, shade and perspective will always
make it beautiful.' [2] Since the most familiar sights are perpetually
altered by the variations in weather, he paints the cathedral pro-
jected against a clear sky, a stormy sky, a clearing sky, a rainbow,
and a double rainbow. But even in these he could still be mindful
of literary relations, as the quotation from Thomson's 'Summer,'
appended to 'Salisbury Cathedral from the Meadows' (exhibited
in 1831), may show:

> As from the face of heaven the scattered clouds
> Tumultuous rove, th' interminable sky
> Sublimer swells, and o'er the world expands
> A purer azure. [3]

He seldom fails to express his tranquil contentment with flat-
ness, rejoicing in the smooth marshiness or fertility of a plain as
much as does Turner in the monstrous majesty of the Alps. Only a
few years after this Ruskin was to teach the English people that
scenic beauty inhered in irregular and rising ground, and that flat
country was not and could not be beautiful — a fantastic notion,
of which the landscapes of Constable and Old Crome are a sufficient
refutation.

The picture of the ruins of Hadleigh Castle [4] reveals a feature
of Constable's work which has perhaps been underestimated by

---

[1] In the South Kensington Museum.
[2] Leslie, 1896, p. 349.
[3] Nine lines in all (1223 ff.) were quoted — inaccurately, as often.
[4] There are two different views of the ruins of Hadleigh Castle. The more familiar
picture, now in the National Gallery, was repeated by the painter in a small water-colour

CONSTABLE.   SALISBURY CATHEDRAL FROM THE FIELDS
From the painting in the Victoria and Albert Museum

critics and historians of art. 'Hadleigh Castle. The Mouth of the Thames — morning after a stormy night' was the painter's chief contribution to the Academy exhibition of 1829, the year of his election. It depicts the solitary fragments of a once-splendid castle (ca. 1231), picturesquely situated on the Essex coast, and commanding a fine view (starred in Baedeker). Undeniably Constable shared the love of ruins so conspicuous in romantic poetry. The crumbling walls, the gathering clouds, the lonely shepherd, the sea-birds in the misty air, 'dreary gleams about the moorland flying'— what are these but the unmistakable stamp of the romantic tradition?

Constable himself illustrated his poetic intention in 'Hadleigh Castle' by quoting lines appropriate to the scene from Thomson's 'Summer.'[1] Leslie remarked long ago, when a knowledge of Thomson's poetry was more wide-spread than it is to-day, that the poet's sentiment was 'finely embodied' in the landscape; but gave no further evidence of the appositeness of the passage. It is from Thomson's hymn to the sun, 'soul of surrounding worlds,' whose radiant fertility, extending through the heavens, invigorates the world, and penetrates even into the bowels of the earth. Even a thing like a ruin, which has no life in it, assumes from the touch of the sun a mimic life:

> The desart joys
> Wildly, through all his melancholy bounds.
> Rude ruins glitter, and the briny deep,
> Seen from some pointed promontory's top,
> Far to the blue horizon's utmost verge,
> Restless, reflects a floating gleam.

The words here which delighted the painter, we may infer, were 'glitter,' as applied to the ruined walls, and the 'floating gleam' reflected from the distant sea. Such atmospheric effects he aspired to reproduce on canvas, often by the use of snowy flakes of white

---

in the possession of Mr. Wayland Williams of New Haven. It is also the one engraved by Lucas for *Constable's English Landscape.*

The other, painted with the ruins in the middle distance, is an oil sketch in the possession of T. W. Bacon, Esq. It is reproduced in Leslie and Shirley (plate 112).

There is a water-colour of Cowdray Castle in Sussex, a ruined manor-house of the sixteenth century. The drawing is in the British Museum.   [1] Lines 165 ff.

CONSTABLE.   HADLEIGH CASTLE

From the engraving by David Lucas in *Constable's English Landscape*

in gay diffusion over the surface of the picture, a mannerism laughed at in his own day — 'Constable's snow' was a derisive phrase — but later to be applauded as a discovery in the rendering of light.

A story told of this picture has contributed to its renown. It is received on the authority of Leslie, who asserts that he was present when the act of desecration was perpetrated:

> I witnessed an amusing scene before this picture at the Academy on one of the varnishing days. Chantrey told Constable its foreground was too cold, and taking his palette from him, he passed a strong glazing of asphaltum all over that part of the picture, and while this was going on, Constable, who stood behind him in some degree of alarm, said to me 'there goes all my dew.' He held in great respect Chantrey's judgment in most matters, but this did not prevent his carefully taking from the picture all that the great sculptor had done for it.[1]

Other pictures reveal the development of Constable's romantic tendency. Sometimes the very titles which he gave to his exhibited works betray it; thus, in 1832, three of the pictures shown were, 'Romantic House, Hampstead,' 'Moonlight,' and 'Jaques and the Wounded Stag.' The last of these, a woodland scene, with a deer drinking from a stream, while Jaques and a companion or two look on from the other side, is accompanied by a quotation, not from *As You Like It*, but from an uninspired poem by Peter Coxe, a glorification of British respectability, *The Social Day*:

> The melancholy, feeling Jaques, whose mind
> Griev'd o'er the wounded weeping hind.[2]

His last picture, now in the museum at Toledo, 'Arundel Mill and Castle,' is another Sussex scene of great charm. On a hillside in

---

[1] Leslie and Shirley, p. 241.

[2] Canto III, p. 71. Although Coxe's verse echoes the feeblest and most prosaic elements of James Thomson in the metrical manner of Walter Scott at his most tiresome, *The Social Day*, published in 1823, is of some importance because of the splendid form in which it was given to the world, a sumptuous volume embellished with over thirty engravings. One of these, representing a windmill on a hillside, is by the elder Landseer after a drawing by Constable (opposite p. 92). Moreover, Coxe mentions the painter by name (p. 59):

> 'Constable, to feeling true,
> Paints Nature's freshness and her hue,
> Studious, like Hobbima, to give,
> And bid the rural landscape live.'

the middle distance are seen the outlines of the nineteenth century castle, to which Constable has lent the romantic grace of Claude.

This emotional interpretation of scenery reaches its full expression in the book of engravings known as *Constable's English Landscape*, a series of twenty-two mezzotints executed by David Lucas under the immediate direction of the painter himself, who was often irritatingly fastidious in criticism and suggestion. The pictures published separately between 1830 and 1832 were entitled, when collected, *Various Subjects of Landscape, characteristic of English Scenery, from Pictures painted by John Constable, R.A.* The book was a kind of *Liber Studiorum*, designed to 'display the phænomena of the chiar'oscuro of Nature,' and 'to promote the love and consequent study of the scenery of our own country, abounding as it does in grandeur and every description of pastoral beauty, and endeared to us by associations of the most powerful kind.' Realistic as he aspired to be in his treatment of Nature, Constable thus acknowledges the influence upon him of local and historical 'associations.' None of the plates is more suffused with such associations than the view of Old Sarum, an engraving of a picture painted in 1829. A long prose description of the scene, published with it, reads in part as follows:

The subject of this plate, which from its barren and deserted character seems to embody the words of the poet, 'Paint me a desolation,' is grand in itself and interesting in its associations, so that no kind of effect could be introduced too striking or too impressive to portray it; and among the various appearances of the elements, we naturally look to the grander phenomena of Nature, as according best with the character of such a scene. Sudden and abrupt appearances of light, thunder clouds, wild autumnal evenings, solemn and shadowy twilights, 'flinging half an image on the straining sight,' with variously tinted clouds, dark, cold, and gray, or ruddy and bright, with transitory gleams of light; even conflicts of the elements, to heighten, if possible, the sentiment which belongs to a subject so awful and impressive.

'*Non enim hic habemus stabilem civitatem.*' The present appearance of Old Sarum, wild, desolate, and dreary, contrasts strongly with its former greatness. This proud and 'towered city,' once giving laws to the whole kingdom — for it was here our earliest parliaments on record were convened — can now be traced but by vast embankments and ditches, tracked only by sheep-walks. 'The plough has passed over it.'

. . . The site now only remains of this once proud and populous city, whose almost impregnable castle and lofty and embattled walls, whose churches, and even every vestige of human habitation have long since passed away. The beautiful imagination of the poet Thomson, when he makes a spot like this the haunt of a shepherd with his flock, happily contrasts the playfulness of peaceful innocence with the horrors of war and bloodshed, of which it was so often the scene:

> Lead me to the mountain's brow,
> Where sits the shepherd on the grassy turf
> Inhaling healthful the descending sun.
> Around him feeds his many-bleating flock,
> Of various cadence; and his sportive lambs,
> This way and that convolved, in friskful glee,
> Their frolics play. And now the sprightly race
> Invites them forth; when swift the signal given
> They start away, and sweep the massy mound
> That runs around the hill, the rampart once
> Of iron war.[1]

If further evidence of this romanticising tendency were needed it could be found in Constable's startling water-colour of Stonehenge, which Mr. Shirley calls 'a most dramatic composition, with a rainbow and clouds so threatening that they are almost garish.'[2] But it is in harmony with Constable's expressed intention to depict the 'grander phænomena of Nature,' the darkening thunder-cloud, the sweeping wind, and the arching rainbow, which beget such melancholy reflections as are found in the quotation used when the picture was exhibited at the Academy in 1836:

The mysterious monument of Stonehenge, standing remote on a bare and boundless heath, as much unconnected with the events of past ages as it is with the uses of the present, carries you back beyond all historical records into the obscurity of a totally unknown period.

Constable's fondness for the subject is shown by the several variants of the drawing.[3]

Constable's last exhibited picture was 'The Cenotaph'; for 'Arundel Mill and Castle' was not shown at the Academy, since it

---

[1] The poetic quotation is from 'Spring,' lines 832 ff. I know of no evidence that Thomson had a particular ruin in mind.

[2] Leslie and Shirley, p. 342.

[3] Leslie and Shirley, plates 147–47b.

CONSTABLE. OLD SARUM

From the painting in the Victoria and Albert Museum

was considered to be unfinished. This picture, begun at the suggestion of Sir George Beaumont many years before, was completed only at the end of Constable's career (1836). In October, 1823, he had paid his first visit to Sir George Beaumont, painter, collector, and patron of artists and poets. The gardens on Sir George's estate, at Cole-Orton, Leicestershire, had been laid out, some fifteen years before that time, according to designs made by William Wordsworth. In 'the dark recesses of the gardens and at the end of one of the walks' Constable found a cenotaph to the memory of Sir Joshua Reynolds, and under the urn some verses by Wordsworth, written at the request of, and in the name of, Sir George. The verses referred to the young trees, planted at the poet's suggestion, so that they might grow in time into a living Gothic aisle. Of this avenue of trees Constable made a drawing during his visit, and not unnaturally gave to the scene the atmosphere of autumn. He had, from the first, intended to make this the subject of a large oil painting, but its completion was long delayed, in part by the death of Sir George in 1827, and in part by Constable's lack of interest in the autumnal atmosphere, which was without that 'exhilarating freshness' which he associated with the spring.

In the catalogue of the exhibition of the Royal Academy for 1836, Constable quoted Wordsworth's entire poem of sixteen lines, the first half of which is as follows:

> Ye lime trees ranged before this hallowed urn
> Shoot forth with lively power at spring's return,
> And be not slow a stately growth to rear
> Of pillars branching off from year to year,
> Till they have framed a darksome aisle,
> Like a recess within that sacred pile[1]
> Where Reynolds 'mid our country's noblest dead,
> In the last sanctity of fame is laid.

The deer in front of the cenotaph, one of the few wild animals to be found in Constable's work, is not in the original drawing;[2] it adds a

---

[1] Westminster Abbey. I give the passage as printed in the Academy catalogue. The fifth line is of course imperfect. It should read, 'Till they have learned to frame a darksome aisle.' Wordsworth seems to have been unaware that Reynolds was buried in the crypt of St. Paul's Cathedral.   [2] Leslie and Shirley, plate 149.

CONSTABLE. STONEHENGE

From the painting in the Victoria and Albert Museum

hint of wildness to the scene which was perhaps no part of the painter's intention and which is scarcely harmonious with the verses. It would be interesting to know whether Wordsworth ever saw the picture.

Constable's admiration of the poetry of Wordsworth [1] is pleasantly indicated by his painting of 'Weymouth Bay,' a coast-scene exhibited in 1817, now in the National Gallery. Among its conspicuous features are the thick, fleecy clouds which hang low over the scene. The shore itself, though austere, is neither hostile nor depressing, but when it re-appeared some years later in the *English Landscape*, it had become dark, threatening and romantic — an alteration in tone which must have been approved by Constable, who superintended the mezzotinting of the plates with the most anxious care. Constable gave a proof of this engraving to Mrs. Leslie, who had greatly admired it.

I shall now [he wrote to her], to give value to the fragment I send you, apply to it a line of Wordsworth:

'This sea in anger and that dismal shore.'

I think of Wordsworth, for on that spot perished his brother in the wreck of the *Abergavenny*.[2]

It is clear that the painter would wish his picture to be examined with emotions similar to those of the reader of Wordsworth's *Elegiac Stanzas on a Picture of Peele Castle in a Storm*, from which the phrase is drawn.

Such are the 'associations' which the painter himself would wish an admirer to find in this landscape. He was no doubt aware that in connecting 'Weymouth Bay' with a well-known line of Wordsworth's he would remind an intelligent spectator not only of the poet's grief for his brother, but also of the fact that the elegy was itself inspired by a picture. Wordsworth had made it clear in the title, 'Stanzas suggested by a Picture of Peele Castle in a Storm,' and by using the picture as an engraved frontispiece in his edition of 1815. Constable must have known the original picture

---

[1] At Cole-Orton, Sir George read aloud from Wordsworth's *Excursion*, and Constable found much to admire in the descriptive passages. One of the preliminary quotations in *Constable's English Landscape* is from the *Thanksgiving Ode*.

[2] Leslie and Shirley, pp. 305–06.

CONSTABLE. THE CENOTAPH
From the painting in the National Gallery, London

well, for it was the work of Sir George Beaumont. Though it is not a masterpiece, it inspired a poem which is among the noblest utterances of William Wordsworth, containing lines as famous as any ever written in praise of the art of painting. The poet conceives of the painter's task as twofold: to express what he sees, and to

> add the gleam,
> The light that never was on sea or land,
> The consecration and the Poet's dream.

In another version of the last line, Wordsworth altered his phrase about the painter's idealising touch to read, 'But borrowed from the youthful Poet's dream,' which though much less beautiful, stresses the relation between painting and poetry. The whole poem shows the use that may be made of a picture by one who knows and loves it. Painting is not merely for moments of serenity, undisturbed by distress and bereavement, and not merely for the heart that lives alone, 'housed in a dream,' without knowledge of the woe of human life. So the fact that Beaumont has chosen to depict a sea in anger and a dismal shore makes his picture of a deeper value:

> O 'tis a passionate Work — yet wise and well,
> Well chosen is the spirit that is here;
> That hulk which labours in the deadly swell,
> This rueful sky, this pageantry of fear!

> And this huge Castle, standing here sublime,
> I love to see the look with which it braves,
> Cased in the unfeeling armour of old time,
> The lightning, the fierce wind, and trampling waves.

Can it be that painting is more than technique? that the artist does not address the eye alone, but extends his influence far into the hidden depths of man's life? It is a creed by no means universally received to-day; but one which would have occasioned no surprise among the artists here discussed. Of their intention and their quest, the official head of the English School, speaking *ex cathedra*, had said,

Whatever abstracts the thoughts from sensual gratifications, whatever teaches us to look for happiness within ourselves, must advance in some measure the dignity of our nature,

CONSTABLE.   WEYMOUTH BAY

Above: from the painting in the National Gallery; below: from an engraving by David
Lucas in *Constable's English Landscape*

and had declared the aim of the painter to be 'to raise the thoughts and extend the views of the spectator.' But Constable goes farther than this. If, during his work, the painter's spirit has been finely touched, the emotions of the spectator will not be left unstirred or lost in a dazed wonder at the artist's skill of hand or clarity of vision. Of the landscape of Gainsborough's at Petworth Constable wrote: 'I now, even now, think of it with tears in my eyes. No feeling of landscape ever equaled it. With particulars he had nothing to do; his object was to deliver a fine sentiment, and he has fully accomplished it.' Such a piece of work he scans 'without comparisons'; for it is unique, like 'every fine thing.' It stills the mind, as it rejoices and invigorates the spirit. It is the artist's consummate act, his final miracle.

INDEX

INDEX